HILLARY'S HISTORY

"An Informative Overview of the Political and Personal
History of Hillary Rodham Clinton"

JOSEPH V. MCCAULEY

<u>Hillary's History – An Informative Overview of the Political and Personal History of Hillary Rodham Clinton.</u>

Published by Joseph V. McCauley, 2124 Pateshall Ct., Virginia Beach, VA. 23464

Copyright 2016

ISBN-10: 1522965262
ISBN-13:
978-1522965268

DEDICATION

To the past, present, and future American Patriots that have and will keep freedom alive.
And to the Wounded Warriors

CONTENTS

ACKNOWLEDGMENTS

Thank you to my wife for your encouragement, grace, and support in the writing of this book.
I love you dearly.

More to come.

1 INTRODUCTION

This historical overview is for the benefit of those Millennials and younger people who, perhaps as first time voters, may not have a personal remembrance of the history of Hillary Clinton and her husband Bill. This book will also help refresh the memories of those, who like me, have experienced the careers of the Clinton couple. There is a saying that if we forget our history we are doomed to repeat it. Too frequently humanity, governments, or a nation's peoples do repeat mistakes of the past. This is because they are either ignorant of that past or if they do have knowledge of it, that retelling was not based on objective truth. Rather, it was based on a biased accounting of the facts to the advantage of one side or the other. Lastly, and perhaps more frighteningly, is when a nation simply chooses to ignore what it can learn from its prior experience. Lessons from our history can help guide our national future.

I have lived through the advent of and on-going personal and political history of Bill and Hillary Clinton. In the pages of this book is an overview of her history. It is a history that again and again, begs the question, "can any of the alleged scandals and wrongdoing be true?" Indeed there should be no judgment without evidence. But the Clintons seem to live and thrive in an environment of political shadows and questionable practices. In the case of Bill and Hillary Clinton there have been many charges and accusations but few convictions. In fact there is only one conviction up to this point in history – the impeachment of Bill Clinton. He was only the second President in U.S. history to receive this dubious distinction. His impeachment was one result of an affair he had as President with a young White House intern, Monica Lewinsky.

The crime that led to his impeachment was that he committed perjury while under oath during a videoed deposition from a lawsuit filed by another woman named Paula Jones. Ms. Jones contended Bill Clinton had physically sexually harassed her. Bill eventually settled out of court for a cool $850,000 paid to Ms. Jones and that case went to the judicial dustbin. However it was found that he did lie about the affair with Ms. Lewinsky. The affair was this: Ms. Lewinsky had oral sex with Bill Clinton. In total she had nine sexual encounters with the President. They took place in the Oval Office of the White House. Under oath, in the deposition he denied the relationship, a federal offense. Bill justified his perjured statement using a contorted explanation of what "sexual relations" were and, adding to it the now famous phase, "it depends on what your definition of 'is' is?" His meaning was that oral sex is not having a "sexual relationship" with someone only sexual intercourse "is" a "sexual relationship." This was in 1998. The impeachment brought to light things such as the President leaving a semen stain on Monica's "blue dress", proof of the encounter. The situation was made even more egregious from the various testimonies given by multiple witnesses aware of the event.

As a father during that time I can tell you it was not a pleasant thing to try and explain what was happening to my two teen-aged boys and a ten-year old. I remember asking myself "how could Bill Clinton be that stupid?" His lack of discretion or respect for the office he held was a poke in the eye to anyone who felt the role he was in deserved a higher level of morality and conduct.

The sordid details were everywhere becoming on-going front-page news on the streets and the nightly news. The big three broadcast stations, ABC, NBC, and CBS were awash with continued revelations about the accusations and the justifications of Clinton's actions.

The impeachment was a high-ratings TV event. This impeachment gave the U.S. public an introduction to a congressional process that had not been used since Andrew Johnson, Lincoln's VP who became President after Lincoln's assassination. Johnson was the first President to be impeached by the Congress. He like Clinton was acquitted by the Senate and remained as President to the conclusion of his one term. Clinton would fulfill the balance of his second term.

Bill's impeachment was a political drama that ended up pointing out the sexual foibles of Congressmen and Senators on both sides of the aisle. Mudslinging and finger pointing abounded, as was a new term in American politics not heard before. The "politics of personal destruction" was a new phrase in the U.S. political lexicon that was introduced by Bill himself. I can recall his speech given after the House of Representatives voted and approved two out of four articles of impeachment against President Clinton in December of 1998. Sanctimoniously, with his Vice President Al Gore at his side, Bill decried the use of this tool in American political discourse. If he was a victim of it one must remember that Bill and his democratic cronies invented it and used it to smear and destroy all the Clinton critics from the 1970s through the full two terms of his Presidency.

Hillary originally defended her husband blaming the accusations on a "vast right wing conspiracy". Eventually the truth that Bill tried to hide came to full light and it led to his impeachment proceedings. He was convicted by the House and later acquitted by the Senate. After all events became public Hillary would declare that Bill had lied to her about the affair, finally having to come clean. I can still recall the video of them coming out of the White House after the impeachment vote. Bill with their dog on a leash, Hillary at his side, and both having their daughter Chelsea holding their hands – but in between them. You could feel the frigid air surrounding them. It must have been humiliating for Hillary to go through that. I wonder if Bill felt that way?

Hillary came out of that affair with very high favorability ratings in the polls. She was after all the wife of an un-faithful husband. She was looked on with sympathy and understanding since Bill had a history of sexual liaisons and adulterous affairs that would make the same reputation held by John F. Kennedy look like a pre-pubescent schoolboy.

As President Bill was known as a "Triangulator". That meant that he would look at both sides of the political spectrum on an issue and then place himself in the political position that benefited him the most. Focus groups (groups that would be polled for their opinions so politicians could see if their policies were favored or not) became a working tool under the Clinton Whitehouse. Bill used this tool skillfully to shift his position on several issues that would be introduced by the Republican House and Senate majorities that came into place in the elections of 1994.

While in office Bill benefited from actions taken by a prior Republican President and on Bill's own ability to re-position himself in the best favorable way to take credit for it. The most significant prior-President benefit that Bill was heir to was the longest period of post war economic growth the U.S. had seen up to that time. This was not due to policies originated in the Clinton Administration per se. Rather Bill rode on the crest of the wave created by the Ronald Reagan tax cuts of the 1980s. These were conservative thinking proposed tax cuts that drastically reduced the tax rates on Americans overall as well as on capital gains. The taxation rates on all income levels went down so dramatically that the action genuinely sparked long-term economic prosperity and growth. People and companies had more money to spend and capital to invest because of the lower tax rates. This boom continued from its original passage in 1981 to the end of 1999 only to burst and finally collapse after the 9/11 attacks on the United States in 2001.

Hillary's history has included the following allegations: questionable financial dealings, misuse of government office for self benefit, the suspicious death of people involved with her and Bill, helping Bill publicly attack and discredit women who accused Bill of sexual harassment and even rape, political manipulation, obfuscation, failure to follow the law, and general untruthfulness. At some point any sane person must ask him or herself, "If there is smoke here, shouldn't there be fire?" Meaning there must be some substance behind the scandals. Even if these accusations had no basis in fact many people just got weary of it. Scandals just kept coming up. How many times do accusations have to come to light only to be backhanded by Hillary as she walks away from them – untouched? She routinely and successfully walks away from them blaming others rather than herself, (I.e. the "vast right-wing conspiracy"). It always seemed there was never enough evidence to bring about legal action. Bill and Hillary just seemed to do things a hairsbreadth outside of legality. The history here is that it was never Bill or Hillary's own personal wrong decision-making that made the nation have to endure another reported scandal.

Hillary is an intelligent woman. Yet she is someone who because of the continued allegations that arise about her, appears to not be above utilizing any position of trust she obtains for her own self-serving purpose. These actions usually come down to the acquisition of one of two things: political power or money. Hillary has reaped handsomely from both.

Both Clintons are skilled political contortionists who time and time again escape scandals that would have jailed a "normal" citizen. Now in her second presidential bid there continues to be new and even more incredulous accusations that have boiled up. Specifically, the alleged mishandling of Hillary's emails as U.S. Secretary of State. This resulted in leaving possible government secrets open and exposed for computer hackers and foreign powers. Then there is also the alleged mis-use of the Clinton Foundation while she was Secretary of State. The allegation being that she used the influence of her State Department position to rake in millions of dollars in speaking fees for her, Bill, and even their daughter Chelsea.

The question of Hillary's presidential bid is not if she is capable. She is a very capable person having won accolades and honors for her own work outside of the sphere of her husband. Her record at Yale Law School, and the body of her writings and work over the years show a person who his able to achieve on her own. She is able to communicate her position on numerous political and social issues with success. Over the course of her lifetime she has seemingly worked sincerely and with good intention regarding the rights of women, children, education, and other political causes she has espoused. But is she capable of being really honest, truthful, and trustworthy? Is she capable of exercising her ambitions based on honorable and worthy motivations rather than self-aggrandizement? Why is there always a second question with Hillary? Why is there always an uncertainty and a wondering if you're being sold a bill of goods that purports to be one good thing when in reality it is meant to achieve something else?

The majority of the American public question her fitness to lead a nation due to the results of her many personal and political actions. You can see that in many of the polls in recent days. For example her foreign policy as Secretary of State has largely been a failure with the end result that the world has become a significantly more dangerous place. Her policies fostered, and the decisions made by the President under which she served have in a very significant way expanded the rise of radical Islamic Jihadism. Those policies and actions have been a disaster that future Presidents will have to address, win, and clean up at tremendous cost. That cost could very probably include the lives of American military personnel as well.

Poll after poll raise the question if she un-trustworthy and corrupt at her core. As of December 2015, 55% of the nation have an unfavorable view of her regarding her being trustworthy. She has credentials that look good on paper: Accomplished College student, Successful Lawyer, First Lady of Arkansas, First Lady of the United

States, U.S. Senator, and U.S. Secretary of State. We would agree that getting elected as a U.S. Senator and staying there is an achievement. But a title bestowed by the benefit of an elected or appointed political office is not an indicator of an honest character. Or, integrity. To the objective viewer the questions remain unanswered. She appears un-genuine, calculating, and chameleon-like in order to try and appear just the opposite of those character traits.

I can sincerely state that I have no ill will toward Bill and Hillary personally but I am cautious. I do however see large-scale mistakes of judgment and a questionable background of conduct. It makes me ask if the history I am experiencing with them shows they are foxes in sheep's clothing. Foxes on the hunt for themselves first and foremost. Foxes who feel they deserve to be in the highest political positions in the land. Their personal and political histories are not something that can be written off with a simple "they all do it." comment. Or, with an "All politicians are crooked, in for themselves, and lie to get and stay in power!" Really? I believe that statement, as sad as it is, is in fact easy to say if you choose to be uniformed, unaware, or un-wanting to ensure that the people who lead our country are worthy of your vote. Conduct matters! Actions taken in private and public matter! The Clinton trend of being caught in the act of a wrongdoing and then blame others displays a deep lack of character.

This then is the reason for this overview book: it is to give a perspective on the actions and decisions of a person who wants to be President of the United States of America. If a person's past and present continue to raise questions of impropriety, wisdom (as with the unsecure server for her State Department emails), integrity, and genuine honesty, should such a person be President? Should that person wanting to be President be voted for simply because the person running is a woman? Although of course absolutely the right woman could certainly do the job. But should we give someone with the historical baggage of Hillary Clinton the Presidency? Would we give Richard Nixon that role again after Watergate? The nation needs to look at her full resume'. The results of her actions from the past are harbingers of what to expect in the future. Now is the time to be informed about Hillary's history. The choice then, is yours!

Lastly, THE PERFECT EXAMPLE!

If you want to see a picture perfect albeit early example of how the Bill and Hillary Clinton Team works watch the 60 Minutes Interview done by Steve Croft with Bill and Hillary from 1992. Here is the link:

https://www.youtube.com/watch?v=2DZyE41T56w#t=354

This was prior to the three-candidate Presidential election in November of that year. Clinton won because of the votes Ross Perot siphoned away from the Republicans in the election. Perot won some 19% of the popular vote taking them away from President H.W. Bush. Had Perot not done that Bush would have won another term. The purpose of the interview mentioned here was to specifically address the accusation that Bill had affairs with other women, and it was pinpointing Gennifer Flowers. Flowers had stated in a tabloid that she and Bill had a long-term affair that lasted over ten years. In the TV interview Bill makes some general statements about how he knew her.

That they had talked on occasion and that he, Bill, had actually talked to Ms. Flowers on the phone while in the presence of Hillary. They were acquaintances, not friends. Then as the questions became more specific and right on target the smoke and mirrors of the answers of the Presidential hopeful and his spouse turned painfully contorted.

This is a grade "A" example of the "emperor has no clothes" experience the American public continually gets from Bill and Hillary Clinton. Their replies to direct questions could not be answered forthrightly because they did not want to be forthright; they wanted him to be President. Ambition appeared to be more important than honesty and integrity. To watch that interview over twenty years later is painful and awkward. You can smell the lawyer's dodge, the conniving answer, and the obfuscation, which repeatedly illustrates a couple that either cannot or will not be truthful.

Compare those contorted and obviously manipulative answers to this quote from George Washington.

"I hope I shall possess firmness and virtue enough to maintain what I consider the most enviable of all titles, the character of an honest man."

George Washington

Should we not expect integrity and honesty from anyone who aspires to the most important political office in our country, Republican or Democrat? I don't care what Party they belong to. I want any candidate to win my vote by their breadth of understanding of the issues of the day. I want to be impressed by their ability to capture the essence of the international and domestic problems, concerns, and needs expressed by the current times and of future necessity. I want to be inspired by words that do inspire showing clarity of mind and a grasp of the issues with solution plans that are well considered and balanced. Richard Nixon lied about Watergate. But he had the integrity to acknowledge that mistake by resigning as President. He spared the country the anguish of an impeachment. Bill Clinton and his wife Hillary did not.

The handling of the email scandal Mrs. Clinton is dealing with most recently shows that the Hillary of 1992 is still alive and well in the Hillary of 2016. You can see this in her replies to reporters. She continues the blaming of others who are conspired against her. She claims the emails she received were not marked classified so she is innocent of handling them incorrectly. She refuses to directly answer questions that should be answered. She is the victim, not the perpetrator, at least in her own mind. It is as if she is saying, "they're bad, I'm good and mis-understood. I did nothing wrong so just accept it. What you see is not really the truth; my version of the situation is the truth."

This then is the tone of her dialog with her fellow Americans. But the facts say otherwise.

No integrity and on-going history of dishonesty.
Where does this leave us? The obvious choice is this:

No to Hillary Clinton for President of the United States.

Joseph V. McCauley

2 HILLARY'S HISTORY - TIMELINE

HILLARY RODHAM CLINTON

Born	October 26, 1947
Where Born	Chicago, Illinois
Religion	Methodist
Father	Hugh Ellsworth Rodam 1911-1993
Mother	Dorothy Emma Howell 1919-2011
Siblings	Hugh Rodham, Tony Rodham
Early Education	National Honor Society Merit finalist - Maine South High School
Original Political Leanings	Conservative

Joseph V. McCauley

1964- Volunteered for Barry Goldwater

1968- Supported Democrat Eugene McCarthy

1968-Attended the Republican National
Convention

1968 - Leaves the Republican Party

1968 - At Wellesley College she organizes a
student strike after the assassination of Martin
Luther King Jr.

College	Wellesley College
Major	Political Science
Year Graduated	1969 (BA) with Honors Political Science

Is first Wellesley College student to deliver a
commencement address

Senior Thesis: Critique of Tactics of
Community Organizer - Saul Alinsky

After graduation travels to Alaska works in a
fish processing cannery in Valdez.

Law School	**Yale Law School**

Interns at law firm of Treuhaft, Walker and Burnstein

(two of four partners were former or then-current Communist Party members)

1971   Begins dating Yale Law student Bill Clinton

Serves on editorial board of the Yale Review of Law and Social Actions (a prestigious role)

Bill Clinton and Hillary Rodham begin living together

1972   Rodham and Clinton campaign for Democrat George McGovern

Receives her Juris Doctor degree from Yale

1973   Writes "Children Under the Law" in the Harvard Educational Review. The article is considered an important piece of legal policy statement regarding how children are represented in relationship to the law and to their parents.

Bill Clinton proposes marriage but is declined.

Becomes a member of the Nixon impeachment inquiry staff in Washington D.C.

Acts as advisor to the House Committee on the Judiciary regarding Watergate.

Richard Nixon Resigns before being impeached.

Hillary fails the District of Columbia bar exam.

1974 Passes the Arkansas Bar exam.

Hillary moves to Fayetteville, Arkansas to be with Bill Clinton.

Hillary joins the faculty of the School of Law at the Univ. of Arkansas, Fayetteville. Teaches on criminal law.

Becomes Director of the Univ of Arkansas Legal Aid Clinic

1975 October 11, 1975 marries Bill Clinton

Retains her maiden name - Hillary Rodham

Moves to Little Rock, Arkansas

Bill Clinton elected as Arkansas Attorney General

1976 Hillary acts as one of the campaign directors of field operations for Jimmy Carter's Presidential campaign

Hillary joins Rose Law Firm

Expertise is patent infringement and intellectual property

Works without fee in child advocacy cases.

President Carter appoints Hillary to Board of Directors of the Legal Service Corporation

Writes papers proposing liberal views of children's rights (Some critics felt Hillary's proposals would overturn parent's rights.)

Hillary co-founds the Arkansas Advocates for Children and Families

1978

Bill Clinton elected Governor of Arkansas, Hillary become First Lady of Arkansas in January 1979

Gov. Clinton appoints Hillary as Chair of the Rural health Advisory Committee.

Becomes first woman full partner of the Rose Law Firm.

1979

> **"CATTLE FUTURES SCANDAL" -** Hillary makes $100,000 profit on a $1,000 investment in cattle futures contracts in 10 months. Investigations show possible questionable future trading practices by Hillary or those representing her.

> **WHITE WATER** - Hillary and Bill invest in the Whitewater Development Corp. That investment will eventually fail while raising questions about conflicts of interest, cronyism and possible illegal financial dealings.

1980

Hillary gives birth to the Clinton's only child - Chelsea - February 27th.

Bill Clinton is defeated in his bid for re-election as Governor of Arkansas.

Bill Clinton re-elected as Governor of Arkansas.

1982   Hillary begins using the name of Hillary Clinton or Mrs. Bill Clinton

Hillary named Chair of the Arkansas Educational Standards Committee

1983   Wins in establishing mandatory teacher testing and state standards for curriculum and classroom sizes.

Named Arkansas Woman of the Year

1984   Named Arkansas Mother of the Year

Continues to practice law at Rose Law firm while serving as First Lady of Arkansas. Makes $200,000 in her last year with firm.

1987 Is Chair of the American Bar Assoc. Commission on Women in the Profession (Ended 1991)

1982 to 1988 Hillary on Board of Directors of the New World Foundation which funded New Left interest groups.

1988

First time named as "one of the most influential lawyers in America" - Named a 2nd time in 1991.

1990 Bill Clinton runs for third team as Governor of Arkansas - is reelected.

Bill accused of having a long-term affair with Gennifer Flowers goes on "60 Minutes" with Hillary denying the affair. He admits to "causing pain in my marriage."

1992 Bill Clinton runs for President of the United States. He wins due to the split of the Republican vote by Ross Perot running as a

3rd party candidate.

Conservative publications begin comparing
Hillary to Shakespeare's "Lady Macbeth"

Hillary Rodham Clinton becomes First Lady
of the United States after Bill Clinton is sworn
in as President.

Becomes the first "First Lady" to have an
office in the West Wing of the White House.
(The wing were official presidential and
governmental business is conducted.)

Hillary assists Bill in the vetting and choosing
of new administration top-level positions and
lower ones.

1993 Hillary recalls having "imaginary discussions"
with Eleanor Roosevelt.

Hillary begins attending a Prayer Group
Fellowship that includes many wives of
Conservative Washington politicians. .

Hillary's father, Hugh Ellsworth Rodham dies
April 7, 1993

January 1993 - Bill Clinton names Hillary to
the Chair of the Task Force on National
Health Care Reform (later called by the media
as "Hillary Care")

(Hillary Care was "a comprehensive proposal
that would require employers to provide
health coverage through individual health
maintenance organizations.")

Hillary Care defeated by both Democrat and
Republican opposition to the plan and failed
to garner enough support for a floor vote in
either House or Senate.

1994

During the 1994 mid-term elections
Republicans gain 53 seats in the House and 7
in the Senate and gain control of both House
and Senate. (This is partly due to American
opposition to Hillary Care.)

Newt Gingrich becomes Speaker of the
House and successfully implements his
"Contract with America"

1995

September 1995 Hillary uses her platform as the First Lady of the United States to stand for women's rights and against abuse at the 4th World Conference on Women in China. This included standing up to China and its policies toward women.

Speaks out against Taliban treatment of women in Afghanistan.

"FILEGATE" scandal breaks in June 1996. Accusations alleged that the Director of the WH Office of Personnel Security received background report files on 700-900 people without authorization to do so. The files included records on previous Republican advisors and administration employees. An investigation held by later Impeachment prosecutor Kenneth Starr exonerates the Clintons due to lack of evidence. Final lawsuit by Judicial Watch ends in dismissal in 2010.

1996

WHITE WATER SCANDAL - After a two year delay records from the Whitewater Development Corporation that Bill and Hillary Clinton had invested in with Jim and Susan McDougal suddenly show up on a table in Hillary's "book room" at the White House. No one knowing how. Whitewater concerned possible conflict of interests on Hillary's part while acting as a lawyer at the Rose law firm.

SUBPOENAED - January of 1996 Hillary becomes the first "First Lady" to be subpoenaed to testify to a Grand Jury investigating the Whitewater scandal.

Works with Senators Orrin Hatch and Ted Kennedy to pass the State Children's Health Insurance Program.

Promotes nationwide immunization for childhood illnesses and mammograms for older women.

1997

Works with Attorney General Janet Reno to create the Office on Violence Against Women at the DOJ.

Achieves what she considers her highest accomplishment as First Lady with the Adoption and Safe Families Act meant to deal with the adoption of special needs children. It also dealt with the need to address the needs of children in abusive families.

1998

> **PRESIDENT CLINTON LIES UNDER OATH** - Bill Clinton already under investigation by Kenneth Starr sees that investigation expanded into impeachment proceedings due to Clinton lying under oath about his extramarital affair with Monica Lewinsky. Hillary calls the allegations part of a "vast right-wing conspiracy". Later Bill admits to Hillary that the affair did take place.

> **PRESIDENT CLINTON IS IMPEACHED**- The House of Representatives votes on two counts to impeach President Clinton. He is acquitted by the Senate.

1999

Hillary decides to run for the New York Senate seat held by retiring Daniel Patrick Moynihan. She had never lived in New York prior to this time, she moves to New York state and buys a house in Chappaqua, NY.

Hillary runs for the Senate and is elected in November of 2000 while George W. Bush is elected President.

2000

The 2000 Presidential election results drags unresolved after election day over the issue of voter count in Florida. It is finally resolved and President Bush is inaugurated.

Hillary is sworn into office as Senator from New York on January 3, 2001

2001
After September 11, 2001 Hillary supports the invasion of Afghanistan. For her the invasion also addresses her position of liberation for the women of Afghanistan from Taliban control while combating terrorism.

Hillary, as Senator, votes for the Patriot Act.

2002
Hillary votes for the Iraq War Resolution

2004   Hillary votes against the Federal Marriage Amendment that would prohibit same-sex marriage.

Hillary co-introduces legislation to increase the size of the US Army by 80,000.

Hillary supports retaining troops in Iraq and is generally opposed by others in the Democratic Party

Hillary starts visits to the troops in Iraq.

2005   Hillary votes against confirmation of John G. Roberts as Chief Justice of the Supreme Court.

Joe Lieberman, Evan Bayh and Hillary introduce the Family Entertainment Projection Act to protect children from inappropriate content in video games.

Hillary votes for the second time against the Firearms Manufacturers Protection Bill. (The bill allows gun manufacturers to not be held accountable for how their products are used. Thus indemnifying gun manufacturers from legal actions due to the use of the weapons they manufacture.)

Hillary for the second time votes against the Federal Marriage Amendment that would prohibit same-sex marriage.

2006

Hillary runs and wins a second term as Senator from New York with 67% of the vote.

Hillary transfers $10 Million from her Senate re-election campaign to her Presidential campaign fund.

Hillary opposes the Iraq War Troop Surge of 2007

Announces she will run for President in 2008

2007

Bill and Hillary election disclosure statements show she and Bill are worth $50M. They earned $100M since 2000 from books, speaking engagements, etc.

Hillary who was originally ahead of Barak Obama in democratic Presidential polls sees her lead reverse. By the end of 2007 Obama is ahead and on track to become the Democratic candidate for President in 2008.

Hillary votes to support the bailout of the U.S. financial system with the Troubled Asset Relief Program - cost $700 Billion

Ted Kennedy endorses Barak Obama.

2008

> **SNIPER FIRE STORY** - Hillary's statements about being under-fire by snipers in a 1996 visit to Bosnia were proved as not true and drew heavy media attention.

After losing significantly to Barak Obama in most of the Democratic primary elections Hillary ends her campaign for the Presidency in June of 2008.

Hillary begins campaigning for Barak Obama and supports him in a speech at the Democratic National Convention for 2008

Hillary ends up in campaign debt and pays off $13Million of it by lending to it from her own resources. All campaign debt was paid by 2013.

Hillary is put forward to be U.S. Secretary of State by President Barak Obama.

Hillary is approved by the Senate Foreign Relations Committee 16-1

She is approved by the Senate in a vote of 94-2 on January 21, 2009 the day after Obama is sworn in as President.

Hillary advocates use of "Smart Power" as a foreign policy for the U.S.

Clinton begins several departmental reforms setting specific objectives for diplomatic missions overseas.

Her goals include utilizing "civilian power" and for empowering women, and for clean and more environmentally friendly food preparation.

2009

Hillary supports Obama's decision to send an additional 21,000 troops to Afghanistan - known as the "Surge". The battle strategy is successful.

Hillary's diplomacy saves a Turkey-Armenian deal that re-established relationships between the two countries.

Hillary uses the "Reset Button" policy to rebuild ties between the U.S. and Russia. Embarrassingly the translation for the word "Reset" in Russian is incorrect. Relations between the countries do improve until Vladimir Putin becomes Russian President in 2012.

Hillary as Secretary of State begins working to impose sanctions on Iran.

Begins travelling to countries all over the world eventually travelling just short of 1 Million miles during her tenure.

2010

Deals with the 2010 Wiki Leaks scandal, which released State Department cables, documents, and assessments of U.S. and other country diplomats.

Arab Spring protests begin in Egypt and Libya. The Mubarak government in Egypt will fall and be replaced with the "Muslim Brotherhood". Mohamed Morsi would be elected President in 2012.

2011

LIBYA - October 2011 Muammar Gaddafi is over thrown and killed in Libya. Libya is judged as a major foreign policy mis-step by the Obama administration and Hillary as Secretary of State. Those policies leave Libya open to radicalization by Isalmist extremists.

September 11, 2012

> **BENGHAZI** - Just two months prior to the 2012 U.S. Presidential elections on September 11, terrorists invade the U.S. diplomatic facility in Benghazi, Libya. Benghazi is not the U.S. embassy but a second U.S. location in Libya. However the U.S. Ambassador is there at the time. He and three others are killed and two U.S. diplomatic locations have buildings set on fire. Ambassador Christopher Stevens is the first U.S. Ambassador killed in the line of duty since 1979.

2012

> The scandal that comes out of the attack is what appears to be a deliberate attempt by Hillary Clinton and President Obama to persuade the American Public that the attacks were based on a "spontaneous" riot reaction to an anti-Muslim video called "Innocence of Muslims". On-going investigations indicate that the attacks were planned in advance to be carried out on the anniversary of the September 11, 2001 attacks. Congressional investigations into Benghazi continue into 2016.

> **BENGHAZI** - January 23, 2013 Hillary testifies to the Benghazi Congressional Committee regarding the 9/11/2012 attacks in Benghazi. On-going events show that original reports on the attack we edited or changed to blame the attack on spontaneous riots due to an anti-Muslim video.

2013

Egyptian President Mohamed Morsi is deposed by a coup d'état in July of 2013 as the Egyptian people rejected the policies, practices and heavy-handed control his government began to exercise. The Military is led by the Minister of Defense, Gen. Abdel Fattah El-Sisi who later becomes Egyptian President in 2014

Hillary resigns as Secretary of State to run for President

Hillary publishes her second memoir, "Hard Choices". Book does not do as well as her first memoir "Living History" published in 2003 for which she received an $8Million advance from the publisher. It sold one million copies in its first month. "Hard Choices" only sells 250,000 copies into late 2015.

2014

Rumors abound that Hillary will make a second run for the Presidency. Her announcement is expected throughout 2014 but is delayed until early 2015.

April 12, 2015 - Hillary announces her candidacy for U.S. President in 2016.

October 13, 2015 – the first Democratic debate puts Hillary up against Senator Bernie Sanders (Independent Socialist Senator for Vermont) , Martin O'Malley (former Gov. of Maryland), Jim Webb (former Senator for Virginia) and Lincoln Chafee (former Gov. of Rhode Island and Senator). By December both Webb and Chafee had dropped out due to significant lack of interest in their campaigns and lack of funding.

2015

> **"EMAIL GATE"** - March 2015, Just prior to her announcing her second Presidential bid Hillary made public the fact that she had used a private email server while Secretary of State instead of the normal secure in-house Dept. of State email services. She noted that she had deleted 30,000 private emails and that at no time had she received or sent secret or classified emails through that server. This came to light due to the fact that the Special Committee on Benghazi had subpoenaed her emails for the investigation the committee was doing regarding the Benghazi incident.

"EMAIL GATE" - By October 2015 an independent FBI investigation was underway to ascertain if Clinton as Secretary of State had mishandled secret or classified U.S. emails. By October the FBI had retrieved several thousands of emails that Hillary had "wiped" from the server. As of November 2015 some 400 emails have been restored by the FBI that were considered secret or classified by their original senders.

In mid-January 2016 the Inspector General assigned to the U.S. Intelligence Community in a letter to a Senate Sub-Committee let it be known that several dozens of Secret, Top-Secret, and ultra-secret (SAP or Special Access Program) emails were found on Hillary's server.

BENGHAZI - On October 22, 2015 Hillary testifies for 11 hours before the Congressional Committee on the Libyan attacks of 9/11/2012. Her emails are mentioned but were not pursued as part of the day's questioning.

Joseph V. McCauley

3 THE SOCIALIST SHIFT OF THE U.S. DEMOCRATIC PARTY

President Andrew Jackson is credited with being the founder of the Democratic Party of the United States. That party has evolved significantly since Jackson's time as it moved into the 21st century. I will start this brief historical review however with another President, Theodore Roosevelt, who became President in 1901. Roosevelt, although a Republican Vice-President and then President was really the model of a President working in modern times to introduce policies and legislation to address the important social issues of the day. Several of Roosevelt's successors were called "Progressive" as he himself is sometimes labeled and many of those men just happened to be Democrats.

PROGRESSIVE VS. SOCIALISM

"Progressive" is a term that is frequently used today by those representing the Democratic Party. It is an alternative descriptor to what the Republicans and many Conservatives would call socialism. Generally since Roosevelt's time Progressive policies have moved away from addressing truly needed reforms to the imposition of "change" that is moving more and more to advance a socialist political agenda. We saw this displayed in the "Change" which was the political anti-George W. Bush buzzword that brought Barak Obama the Presidency in 2008. This political shift includes the socialist goal of the redistribution of wealth. There is a momentum in the Democratic Party today to shift more power and control over the lives of

Americans to a central Federal government and away from both the states and the individual citizen.

THE DEMOCRATIC PARTY SHIFT TO SOCIALISM

What I hope to illustrate here is to show that as the Democratic Party went through the 20th century into the 21st, it shifted to policies that were not what I would define as fitting the historical "Progressive" playbook. By "historical Progressive" I mean the addressing of social issues working collectively and collaboratively within Congress and with the President. Those kinds of political collaborations of course did not happen all the time. However historically here in the U.S there has been no intent to socially control Americans, as would be the result for the people of Russia after the Communist Revolution there in 1917. There was still within U.S. political dialogue an ability to work for successful compromise to benefit the majority of Americans. A good example of this being the tax cut deal made between President Reagan and Thomas "Tip" O'Neill the Speaker of the House in 1982. American social issues could be addressed with the opposing parties working things out within the context of the three-part U.S. system of federal government. They sought a common ground for a common good. Now, under the Administration of the 21st Century's first Democratic President we are seeing strong socialist based policies pushed through Congress without the debate or discussion to get a consensus and the most useful and cost effective legislation.

It is particularly in the implementation of social policy under President Barak Obama that we see Democrats introduce policies and cultural changes that have been put in place, as interpreted by many observers, by not dealing honestly with the American public. Examples? President Obama's lying to the American people about Obama Care, Congressional political gamesmanship, deception, and preventing honest political give-and-take on issues (such the vote on Obama Care- see below) have taken place. These have demonstrated that the Democratic Party of the early 21st century does not feel it can get what IT wants while being fair and square with the American electorate.

THEODORE ROOSEVELT

Let us begin then by using Theodore Roosevelt as our starting example. What were some of the social issues his administration addressed? They included ending child labor abuses and the need for labor unions to give workers a voice against the control of business monopolies. He addressed the need for centralized health control standards by the federal government with his establishing of Dept. of Health food inspectors. He used his office to confront government cronyism, and business trusts that would monopolize their industries. Those monopolies sought to control the cost and flow of goods and services in such a way as to prevent competitors from entering those businesses. All this was being done by those monopolies without any concern to provide a genuine benefit to the U.S. Public by bringing lower prices, alternative products or services to that public. Roosevelt began his Reformist career as the New York City Police commissioner in 1894. The NYPD at the time had a reputation of looking the other way from crime, had no standards of conduct for all ranks in the department, or for the hiring of new recruits. Roosevelt in his usual impassioned and impetuous way would actually go out at night or between shift changes to see just what the officers on the beat were doing and if they were in fact – on duty. He would often find the officers asleep. TR began training and inspections in firearms and standards for physical fitness. He also stopped the hiring of officers based on their political party, a typical cronyism practice of the day. With the advent of the telephone becoming more common he had them installed in the New York City Police precinct stations. Thus he improved the communications, responsiveness, and effectiveness of the police force. He generally implemented standards where none existed. He held both officers and police commissions accountable for integrity, honesty, and genuine service to the public. His exploits and reforms were well broadcast in the newspapers of the day further cementing his reputation as a solid reformer for public good. As he created enemies he also was garnering respect for the reforms that would expand Roosevelt's reputation outside of New York City.

Roosevelt's championship of reform came from a strong moral core that he obtained from his father, also named Theodore. The senior Roosevelt was known among his highly successful businessman peers as "Lionheart". This was because of his generosity toward the poor and under privileged in New York at the time. He was particularly attuned to the suffering of poor children. There is the story of the senior Roosevelt throwing a dinner party for all of his rich friends. After being called to the dining table they sat with him waiting for the food to arrive.

However TR's father used the occasion for a more noble cause than just eating. Before dinner was served he had his servants open the doors to the room and in came a large group of these underprivileged and destitute children. With their entrance Roosevelt then pointed out to his friends the hardships and needs of the children and their families. Finally he called on his friends to help by giving to the poor and needy like those children present with them that evening.

Theodore the younger would be motivated to continue such work by the example of his father. He would be equally as strong and as passionate in his work as a conservationist. Teddy from a child began to develop a deep knowledge and understanding of nature, birds, and a wide variety of animals. Largely self-educated by his reading he would become an acknowledged expert and naturalist. Even as a young boy he could imitate numerous birdcalls and whistles. As President he would by legislation and executive order set aside thousands of acres of American wilderness as national parks. This was a forward-looking series of actions that has preserved those parks for all generations of Americans up to the present day.

The majority of Theodore Roosevelt's presidency would be remembered for his direct action to get things done for the American people using his office as President. He did break up monopolies or trusts that he considered as harmful to the U.S. public due to their significant control over large parts of the U.S. economy. In 1902 he skillfully prevented a countrywide coal strike concluding it with the resolute statement that he wanted "a fair deal for every man." He also worked for and succeeded in exercising government control over railroad fees that would harm interstate commerce. In 1905 he earned and won the Nobel Peace Prize for the settlement he negotiated

personally that ended the Russo-Japanese War. In 1906 he
implemented Meat, Drug, and Food Acts that would provide for
government inspection of foods distributed across the country
and prevent false labeling of many foodstuffs and drugs.

Theodore Roosevelt was a man who worked for positive and
necessary change but in the context of the common good. He
acted with integrity and the force of right. He did not seek nor
was his intention to have the intimidation of big government
control the hearts, minds, and lives of Americans. He was no
socialist. He was the champion for the right of a person to
achieve on his or her own. It is the attitude, motivation, and the
way policies are achieved that makes these Presidential actions
either liberty enhancing or socialist controlling. Roosevelt was
not working to have the federal government control people's
lives. He wanted that "fair deal for every man" to emanate from
the government with that government setting the playing field to
facilitate that goal.

So we see in TR a man who was working from an inner
conviction to do good for others outside of himself. His father's
strong Christian beliefs as well as his own were the foundation of
where President Roosevelt began, worked, and stayed in the
reforms he felt were needed. As TR himself said of his father's
imprint on his own life, **"My father, Theodore Roosevelt, was
the best man I ever knew. He combined strength and
courage with gentleness, tenderness, and great
unselfishness. He would not tolerate in us children
selfishness or cruelty, idleness, cowardice, or
untruthfulness."** President Roosevelt never attempted to

deceive the people. His moral inner man would not tolerate deliberately lying to achieve his end. Truth was part of what made winning the noble cause noble. He felt that he had to do things honestly presenting the facts and dealing with them in a straightforward manner.

Social issues in the same genre as Roosevelt's have come up over the years, which had to be addressed, such as the much-needed de-segregation in the 1960s. But today, the Democratic Party has migrated into policies that seek to control people down to the very individual level.

Under President Obama the federal government has turned into a political " Intimidator". It forced the American public to buy Government mandated health insurance and to accept abortion contrary to a business's or person's individually held sincere religious beliefs. Obama Care specifically demands compliancy to its beliefs and policies or face a financial penalty. That is not "Progressive". It is socialism enforced by financial tyranny.

I contend that for the Democrats the shift in addressing social issues has moved from one of dialogue and discussion to achieve a mutually agreed-to and desired benefit, to one of dominance and control. It is now the heart of the way the Democratic Party does things. Through his unconstitutional executive orders it is the way President Obama does things. Since he cannot get Congress to agree with him now that the Republicans control both the House and Senate he will "rule" by Presidential decree, i.e. his executive orders.

We can see that Theodore Roosevelt's Democratic Presidential successors like Woodrow Wilson, Franklin Roosevelt, Harry Truman, John F. Kennedy and Lyndon Johnson each had their own social issues of their day to deal with and resolve. Wilson had a world war, Franklin Roosevelt had to confront and turn-a-round a financial abyss that is still called the "Great Depression" and then a second world war. Truman had to end that war and guide America into a "Cold War" with the world's then second nuclear power. John F. Kennedy had to confront that same world power when it threatened the shores of the United States itself. He and Lyndon Johnson would both deal with de-segregation. Let's look in more detail at what these Presidents did.

WOODROW WILSON

President Wilson introduced the Federal Reserve, a progressive act that created a series of twelve Federal Reserve Banks given authority to issue Federal Reserve notes. Its main purpose was to establish more effective oversight and stability of the banking industry in the United States. The Federal Reserve also provided services to its member banks meant to standardize actions such as check clearing and collection. Its overall intention, as a newspaper of the time stated, was to be "a series of constructive acts to aid business." Wilson introduced the personal income tax – for good or ill depending on your point of view. He also continued to work on social issues related to child labor. Wilson, after maneuvering through opposition by members of his own Democratic party put his support behind the 19th Amendment, which gave women the right to vote. I would call that a needed and successful "Progressive" policy. He supported the British Balfour Declaration of 1919, which allowed Jews to return to their homeland of Israel.

FRANKLIN ROOSEVELT

Franklin Roosevelt attempted to utilize the government's greater resources and capabilities to turn a financially wounded country around. The Depression was at its height during his Presidency. His actions such as the "CCC" or Civilian Conservation Corp introduced federally funded programs that gave people work such as the building of roads and public buildings. With the start of World War II Franklin Roosevelt had the will, the communications skill, and administrative capabilities to put the right people in the right places to win a global war. FDR inspired the nation with his actions in defense of the country and the determination of his words that united the country behind him. FDR's programs were not socialism. They were however socially responsible as the U.S. government worked to revitalize and pull the country out of the impacts of its financial collapse in 1929. The goal was to get the nation back on its financial footing but not to control the citizenry. Even the "Social Security" program had as its intention to assist the individual citizen in preparing for their older years. For its time it was an appropriate program.

HARRY TRUMAN

Harry Truman, the next Democratic President finished the work FDR had begun in the defeat of the Axis powers of Germany, Japan, and Italy. The defeat of Germany was a foregone conclusion when Truman became President after the death of FDR on April 12, 1945.

Germany surrendered the next month. Truman authorized the
use of the atomic bomb so as to spare the loss of an estimated
one million American soldiers by a direct invasion of Japan. He
brought an end to the war on September 2, 1945. After the War
Truman's administration began some of the most remembered
international social programs of its time. First, through Truman
the United Nations was established in 1946. It turned out to be a
better success than its spiritual predecessor, the League of
Nations after World War I. This was followed by one of the
most generous and selfless act of any government. It was the
Marshall Plan. Truman used that plan and spent $13 Billion to
rebuild Europe including the former Axis partners of Germany
and Italy. Then the U.S. helped rebuild Japan. When the
Russians assumed control of East Berlin in 1948 they cut off its
road and railway accesses thus separating Berlin from the rest of
Europe. Truman in concert with the British, Canadian,
Australian, and New Zealand governments authorized an airlift to
provide food and fuel to the East Berliners. Within the one-year
of its operation from June of 1948 to May of 1949 the airlifts flew
over 200,000 missions and dropped 8,893 tons of food to the
blockaded city. The Russians did not oppose the airlifts through
military action since they did not want to start another war.
Russia eventually rescinded the blockade. Domestically, Truman,
as Commander-In-Chief, also introduced executive actions to
begin racial integration of the military. Civil Rights were a core
issue for him. By his Executive Orders to integrate the American
military he incentivized what would flower into the Black Civil
Rights movement of the 1960s.

JOHN F. KENNEDY

John F. Kennedy would be the President of history during one of the key periods at the start of the Black Civil Rights movement. Kennedy met with leaders like Martin Luther King Jr. and others sharing their desire for black civil rights and integration. Kennedy's brother Robert would, as the Attorney General, provide legal support and protection to the Civil Rights demonstrators during the short three-year term of John Kennedy. Lyndon Johnson, Kennedy's successor and a Southerner, would be the next Democrat who would pick up the Civil Rights mantle.

Working with key Republican leaders and in spite of strong segregationist opposition within his own Democratic Party Johnson obtained the support he needed to pass his signature Civil Rights Bill. He signed it into law as the Civil Rights Act of 1964, with Dr. King present at the signing. It was a major step forward to America fulfilling the principles stated in the Declaration of Independence.

LYNDON B. JOHNSON – THE WAR ON POVERTY

In the mid-1960s Johnson introduced a well-intentioned but eventually failed public law, which came to be known as the "War on Poverty". Its plan was to utilize federal programs and funds to *"not only relieve the symptom of poverty, but to cure it, and above all, to prevent it."* as President Johnson stated. It was at this moment in time that the shift to socialist based policies by the Democratic Party and its future Presidents began. It was birthed from the assumption that Government based programs and forced wealth redistribution could do something to bring prosperity in place of poverty for its citizens. This was the antithesis

of implementing government policies that would create an
environment that would allow U.S. capitalism to expand the
economy and facilitate job creation. Programs that still exist
today such as Job Corp and Head Start are the remains of that
legislation. The law failed over time because of its dependence
on the welfare state and the central government to be the source
of financial provision for the citizens. It was the giving away of
money without a central coordination of the program to make it
truly effective as Dr. Martin Luther King Jr. later stated. This was
the federal government, instead of creating an environment for
business to flourish through capitalism and thus create jobs,
becoming the giver of free money that required little to no work,
accountability, or responsibility.

The Johnson law did have some positive impacts initially but not
in the long term. Finally recognizing the "War on Poverty" as
failed in 1996, Bill Clinton signed a law that ended the welfare
aspects of the Johnson Act. The change called for work
requirements, accountability, and other actions that would
eventually move those receiving aid to get work and be sustained
without government assistance. For Clinton this change was
motivated by a newly Republican controlled Congress that would
push for welfare reform big time. Since the end of Johnson's
Presidency the Cato Institute has estimated that there has been
almost $19 Trillion spent on welfare programs. The results of
which have produced nominal shifts from the poverty
percentages found under the Johnson Administration. Thus a
precedent for non-wartime big government spending was
launched. From this the Democrats developed the thinking that

government control of the economy, the lives, and money of the American people was the solution to America's social problems. This is big government telling you that it knows better than you and will take what you have to implement what it thinks best. Hello socialism!

SOCIALST = DEMOCRAT?

This then is the major theme of the shift that has taken place in the Democratic Party of the early 21st century. It has been a march towards a socialist government. As I stated earlier Socialism is a political theory and system that advocates a strong central government that controls at all levels of society. These controls can include businesses, welfare programs, child rearing, providing health and education programs and their funding like as is seen in Scandinavia. Utilizing high taxation rates socialism assumes that the government will pay for and thus control everything you do from cradle to grave. With the advent of the Obama administration we have seen the largest and most egregious example of this trend, Obama Care.

With Obama Care Democrats now appear to not care about political dialog and debate to develop the best policies and I might add the most cost effective ones to benefit Americans. BIG government spending is now standard operating procedure in Democrat policies. Through that spending the Party's goal is to exercise political mandates that will control Americans. Socialism is a political philosophy that is growing in favor with the Democratic voter base. Indeed a recent Gallop Poll (June 2015) stated that 59% of Democrats showed a willingness to vote for a Socialist versus 26% of Republicans and 49% of Independents. As an example of how socialist policies are being implemented by Democrats I will focus for this book on one issue, Obama Care.

OBAMA ADMINISTRATION MIS-REPRESENTATION OF OBAMA CARE

Obama Care or the Affordable Care Act signed into law in 2010 is an example of socialism exercised at the expense of liberty and freedom of choice. The intention of Obama Care was to provide health insurance coverage to some 45 million Americans who did not have it, or could not buy it due to poverty, or it not being available through employers. This was a well-intentioned program. However the way it was made law shows a Democratic Party and a President who know they will not get what they want if they honestly bring an overtly socialist agenda before the American people. What made this program so egregious was the way it was presented and then politically manipulated to pass Congress. Here then is a history of some of the lies and manipulations that were taken to pass Obama Care.

OBAMA CARE – THE PRESIDENT LIES ABOUT KEEPING HEALTH CARE PLANS

First President Obama misled the American public by his continued statement that "if you have a doctor you can keep your doctor." or, "if you have a plan you can keep your plan." He added that it would save the average family $2,500 a year in health premium costs. Americans took those statements as a pledge that they would not lose what they currently had if they wanted to keep the health care providers they were using. It became fully evident after the law's passage that Obama misled in an attempt to create an atmosphere of acceptance for his proposed legislation.

OBAMA CARE – PROMISES NOT KEPT – NEGATIVE IMPACT ON BUSINESS AND PEOPLE

Secondly, the legislation once passed and in implementation actually did force many employers to change their plans due to the new regulations from that law. Employers often had to reduce their work force so as to not have to pay penalties the law required. The law mandated employers to give health benefits in those companies that had more than 50 employees or if an employee worked over 30 hours a week. People who were working less than 40 hours found their hours significantly cut so that employers could call them part-time and not be forced to provide healthcare as required by the law. Hiring was reduced and people were laid off so that small businesses would staff at less than the 50-employee requirement. People, by the thousands, did lose their plans and had to shift to other plans. The ones mandated by the federal government, led by the Democrats. Additionally medical premiums were ridiculously variable. I know personally of one man who took out a medical plan on the Obama Care web site and ended up paying $400 per month for his coverage. His wife, whom he had to set up as her own account because she made so much less than he got the same level of coverage for just $1. , per month. He was subsidizing her with his high monthly premiums. Let us also add to this the humiliating and embarrassing flawed rollouts of the Obama Care web sites that proved to be un-secure, poorly engineered, and confusing to users. The web site problems had to be corrected over time.

Here then was social re-engineering at its worst. If you had more income then you had to pay more than those with a lesser income. The cost burden for their health care was transferred to you the higher-wage earner. This was not equality it was forced "taking from the rich to give to the poor". A perverse "Robin Hood" mentality that is at the core of socialism. This legislation was one of the biggest forced redistributions of wealth in American history. Not even FDR's social security program was like this. These kinds of actions are also in line with the Obama administration's goal to end "income inequality", which is the discrepancy between high wage earners and low. Neither of these approaches are right or fair. The attempt by the federal government to end income "inequality" is just the "war on poverty" using a new political lexicon. In America you get what you can earn because you have the skill set and/or expertise that others will pay for appropriately in the market place.

Is it the government's role to "fix" income inequality?

That's socialism speak!

DEMOCRATIC HOUSE AND SENATE "CHANGE THE RULES" TO PASS OBAMA CARE

Thirdly, I bring up the deceptive sleight of hand done by the Democratically controlled House and Senate that actually got Obama Care passed WITHOUT a single Republican vote for it. I quote here from a Blog- article by conservative talk show host Brian Sussman (Station KSFO) from November of 2013 and re-posted to his blog in June of 2015. It simply and briefly outlines the contortions the Democratic controlled Congress went through to pass this bill. This was the bill that the then Speaker of the House, Nancy Pelosi, spoke of when she said, "We'll have to pass it to see what's in it." What?! That does not now nor did it then sound logical or make sense at all. The Congress should know what's in a bill before it is voted on. Listen to how this legislation got passed. It wasn't through debate, dialog, or an attempt to get the best law through mutual agreement. It was forced through instead by Democratic congressional leadership political manipulation of the system.

Here's Sussman's article: (Used by permission.)

June 26, 2015

I originally posted this piece on November 21, 2013. However after yesterday's Supreme Court ruling it began trending, so I'm reposting it:

It was the trickiest legislative move ever accomplished in the Congress. Here's my best play-by-play:

Obamacare was signed into law in March 2010. If you recall, Nancy Pelosi's Democratic majority in the House of Representatives was unable to pass their version of a healthcare law. Because all revenue bills have to originate in the House, the Senate found a bill that met those qualifications: HR3590, a military housing bill. They essentially stripped the bill of its original language and turned it into the Patient Protection and Affordable Care Act (PPACA), aka Obamacare.

The Senate at that time had 60 Democrats, just enough to pass Obamacare.

However after the bill passed the Senate, Democrat Senator Ted Kennedy died. In his place, Massachusetts elected Republican Scott Brown. That meant that if the House made any changes to the bill the Senate wouldn't have the necessary number of votes to pass the amended bill (because they knew no Republicans would vote for Obamacare). So Senate Leader Harry Reid cut a deal with Pelosi: the House would pass the Senate bill without any changes if the Senate agreed to pass a separate bill by the House that made changes to the Senate version of Obamacare. This second bill was called the Reconciliation Act of 2010. So the House passed PPACA, the Senate bill, as well as their Reconciliation Act. At this point PPACA was ready for the President to sign, but the Senate still needed to pass the Reconciliation Act from the House.

Confused?

We all were.

And it got worse.

Remember that the Senate only had 59 votes to pass the Reconciliation Act since Republican Scott Brown replaced Democrat Ted Kennedy. Therefore in order to pass the Act Senate Democrats decided to change the rules. They declared that they could use the "Reconciliation Rule (this is a different "reconciliation" than the House bill). This rule was only supposed to be used for budget item approvals so that such items could be passed with only 51 votes in the Senate, not the usual 60. Reconciliation was never intended to be used for legislation of the magnitude of Obamacare. But that didn't stop them.

So both of the "Acts" were able to pass both houses of Congress and sent to President Obama for his signature without a single Republican vote in favor of the legislation. The American system of governance was shafted. To quote Democrat Rep. Alcee Hastings of the House Rules Committee during the bill process: "We're making up the rules as we go along."

http://www.briansussman.com/politics/how-obamacare-became-law/

Wow!

JONATHAN GRUBER – THE ARCHITECH OF OBAMA CARE- "AMERICANS ARE STUPID. "

In 2014 a political firestorm broke out due to the comments of Jonathan Gruber a Professor of Economics from M.I.T and the proclaimed "Architect of the Affordable Care Act" (Obama Care). From 2010 to 2013 Gruber had spoken at numerous events about the ACA. In the videos from those events Gruber spoke strongly about how the ACA was crafted and "written in a tortured way" to hide the fact that the ACA would create a way in which "healthy people pay in and sick people get money." He also stated that this rank deception was done to make sure the bill passed due to the "stupidity of the American voter." This MIT Professor was letting the whole world know that the bill was written in such a way as to hide the truth of what it really contained. This architect of the health care plan had previously helped then Massachusetts Governor, Mitt Romney, create that state's single payer health plan in 2006. That assignment would lead to his selection as the contractor who would help develop Obama's plan.

SOCIALIST POLITICAL STRONG ARMING OF OBAMA CARE

The other aspect of Obama Care was its far left hard line liberal position on abortion. Since its passage into law in 2010 we have seen lawsuits where companies and even a convent of Nuns had to go to court to prevent their organizations from having to follow the Obama Care mandates to pay for abortion services. This mandate for Obama Care included a provision forcing the payment for a "morning after" pill, which would prevent conception by chemical intervention with the fertilization process. Those opposing this were people of sincere religious faith that were opposed to abortion based on their faith. Religious freedom is part of the Constitution and is a primary founding liberty of this country. Where did this Democrat oppositional stance to religion come from? From within the Party. Example?

Very well I remember the Democratic Party Convention of 2012. During that session, after the committee drafting their platform had removed the mention of "God" from it there was a dramatic and explosive brawl on the floor of the convention. Many of the delegates wanted to put "God" back in. There were shouts and catcalls as the TV cameras focused on blocks of people who were vocally and loudly expressing their disdain for any attempt to put the mention of" God" back in to the platform document. Eventually it was restored by floor vote back in to that platform. They had to vote to include "God" in their platform? What does such an event say about a political party's moral core? This demonstration made the Democratic Party appear very anti-faith and anti-religious freedom.

Seriously, we must ask, what do threats to a group of Nuns for not wanting to comply with Obama Care say about the Democratic Party, its intentions, and about Mr. Obama himself? He could have interceded in that situation had he wanted to. He did not. The Supreme Court will hear the case in March of 2016.

THE FUTURE SOCIALIST TREND

The Nun's story is symptomatic of the lack of tolerance the leftist-socialist Democratic Party is moving to. Its goal is to control or remove liberties. They are the Party that speaks a good story about tolerance but who are not willing to exercise tolerance towards those who oppose its policies. Under President Obama and the Democrats there is no room for debate or compromise. The use of the Federal Government's powers to "force" people into compliancy is typified in the implementation of Obama Care. Is Obama Care a good idea? On the surface it is. But it could have been engineered in a totally different way if the Democrats were not thinking as socialists. This could have been done on a more effective scale by focusing on just those people without health insurance and crafting a smaller and smarter solution. A business team working with insurance companies and Congress to target that group of uninsured people could have achieved the results of Obama Care without having to re-engineer a huge part of the economy.

The way Obama Care was created and implemented can be seen in hindsight as an action that really did screw up the health care plans millions of Americans were already happy with. Neither did businesses have to be penalized and their resources for further investment stolen because of a socialist designed program. It was a program that could have been far better in design if given more time, real debate, and if a business-like review of the need had been exercised. With, I might add, the goal of making it cost effective.

If not stopped under Hillary Clinton this kind of socialist expansionism will continue. She will seek more control over Americans in a variety of ways. I also see her having a particular goal on actions that would lead to the weakening or removal of the second amendment right to bear arms. She is anti-gun rights.

It would also appear Hillary is against religious freedoms!

Example: Hillary said the following in a recent speech at the 6th annual Women in the World Summit regarding abortion:

"Far too many women are denied access to reproductive health care and safe childbirth, and laws don't count for much if they're not enforced. Rights have to exist in practice — not just on paper," "Laws have to be backed up with resources and political will," she explained. "And deep-seated cultural codes, religious beliefs and structural biases have to be changed..."

She will change the "deep seated ...religious beliefs" of whom? All Americans? Or just those who don't agree with her?

If her strongest alternative democratic Presidential candidate, Bernie Sanders, an avowed socialist, were elected President he would be even worse if not constrained by a Republican Congress.

Is a socialist state really what anyone should vote for? The Russian Communist Empire collapsed because of its ultra-socialist government and restrictions on its people. That's why the Berlin Wall finally came down.

What did the fall of communism illustrate?

SOCIALISM DOESN'T WORK!

To quote Winston Churchill:

"Socialism is a philosophy of failure, the creed of ignorance, and the gospel of envy, its inherent virtue is the equal sharing of misery."

Freedom, the Constitution, and American Capitalism are what made this country strong and great. The "Change" that came through the Administration of Barak Obama has given the citizens of America an $8 Trillion increase in the national debt, a poorly crafted health care reform, and an assault on the second amendment and religious freedoms.

A vote for Hillary Clinton or any Democratic Presidential candidate in 2016 is a step towards greater Federal government socialist control of your life and mine. We cannot let that happen.

Joseph V. McCauley

4 HILLARY AS U.S. SENATOR

Hillary Clinton has worked hard to distinguish herself from her husband and from the roles of past U.S. First Ladies. She has done this by her long-term direct involvement in the politics of the United States. She always saw herself as something more than a second string, behind-the-scenes "Wife and Mother". She said she was inspired to an activist role by the example Eleanor Roosevelt displayed after the death of FDR. Her own personal ambition motivated her to follow her goal to achieve the highest political office in the U.S., the Presidency.

By necessity Hillary knew she had to achieve this goal over time. Thus requiring her to build up her credibility and political resume. Being First Lady of the United States is a result of marriage and a husband's political success. She needed to step beyond that role to something new that would allow her to move on to the Presidency. As one of the means to achieve that and to give herself deeper political credentials Hillary decided to run for the U.S. Senate in 2000. She did that by seeking the seat left by departing New York Senator Patrick Moynihan. She eventually saw her tenure as First Lady end on January 20 of 2001 when George W. Bush replaced Bill Clinton as President. But that was not before she had already stepped into her new political role as a U.S. Senator earlier in the month on January 3, 2001.

Her Senate run began when Bill and Hillary purchased a house in Chappaqua, New York just north of New York City in 1999. Hillary was accused of carpet bagging since she had only lived in Washington D.C. or Arkansas up to that time. She had never been a resident of

New York State. A fact that was met with some skepticism and distain by many New York state residents. This was not anything new as Robert Kennedy (JFK's brother) had made similar move years earlier in 1964. Hillary made history by being the only First Lady ever to win an elected political office. Her election in many ways was a foregone conclusion since she was running in a very "blue" and liberal state.

She was personally popular at that time due to the nation-wide sympathy she received in the wake of her husband Bill's affair with Monica Lewinsky and his impeachment. In the election itself her original opponent, New York Mayor Rudy Giuliani, although personally popular had to withdraw from the race due to a diagnosis of prostate cancer. Giuliani would later be moved back into the national spotlight in the aftermath of the 9/11/2001 terrorist attacks on New York City while he was Mayor. After Giuliani bowed out the Republicans replaced him with Rick Lazio who was a Republican member of the House for New York. Hillary defeated Lazio roundly getting 55 percent of the vote while Lazio got 43 percent. Her platform called for her to bring some 200,000 jobs into New York over her term as Senator. New Yorkers are still waiting. Once the announcement that she was running for the Senate was made Hillary and her election team threw themselves into non-stop electioneering. She visited every county in New York State on "listening-tours" in usually small town-hall kinds of settings.

To Hillary's credit after she became a Senator and after the 9/11 attacks she worked with great effort to get the funding for the rebuilding of the now fallen Twin-Towers of the World Trade

Center, the buildings targeted in the 9/11 attacks. She worked with Senator Charles Schumer to obtain $21 Billion in funding to rebuild the World Trade Center site. Eventually a single tower, which contains a memorial museum to the 9/11 attacks, was completed and opened in 2014; 13 years after the attacks and 5 years after Hillary left the Senate.

Hillary's record in the Senate was not an impressive one. While there she was a member of several committees. None of which in and of themselves gave her any real public facing notoriety. Two of the committees were the Senate Armed Services Committee and the Committee on Health, Labor, and Pensions. Neither were high-profile committees that would place her with frequency in the nightly news. Her record in the Senate showed that she introduced 377 bills in eight years. 323 of those bills were stopped in committee going nowhere producing an 85.6% failure rate or "extremely poor" rating according to GovTrack. Ten of her bills were enacted into law while she did co-sponsor 1,858 bills.

I remember actually seeing Hillary Clinton outside the Capitol Building in May of 2006. I was on an "American Heritage" tour of Plymouth and Boston, Massachusetts, and Washington D.C. for the Christian School on whose advisory board I was serving. The tour was led by the late Rev. Peter Marshall Jr., (1940-2010) the son of the famous Senate Chaplain, Peter Marshall Sr. (1902-1949). Hillary was outside the Senate Building doing what we had just done with Senator John Thune, having a photo shoot with some folks probably from her state, mostly kids, as was our high school tour. It was interesting to actually see this woman who had been the vortex of so much positive and negative history.

Hillary was serving as the U.S. Secretary of State when the Democratically controlled Congress passed the Obama Care medical bill.

GUN RIGHTS

Hillary has never been pro-gun rights. We can see this reflected in her voting record by noting that she was for holding gun manufacturers responsible for any mis-use of the products they manufactured. The key of course is defining what "mis-use" would mean. It meant criminal or terrorist acts. Simply put she is for allowing gun manufacturers to be sued due to the fact that the perpetrator of a crime or terrorist act had used one of their products. This is like holding auto manufactures liable when anyone driving their products kills people – ridiculous! Holding gun manufacturers legally responsible for the use of their weapons by the purchasers of those products was and is a policy strongly opposed by individual gun owners, the NRA, and the Republican Party in general. Hillary has always pushed for gun controls at the federal level and uses her opposition to the NRA as a political fund raising tool.

TERRORISM

With Hillary's Senate first term starting in January 2001 she found herself as part of that body during and after the September 11, 2011 Islamic Jihadist attacks planned by Usama Bin Laden. Generally her terrorism votes during that period fell in line with the attitude and mood of the country at that time. This was, that the U.S. needed to act and act quickly to deal with the most recent terrorist threat but also to deal with future threats. To that end on October 25, 2001 Hillary voted for the Patriot Act. That act according to the summary at VoteSmart.Org was *"a bill that grants law enforcement more authority to search homes, tap phone lines, and track Internet use of those suspected of terrorism."* This bill passed the House and Senate with non-opposition. It would have very likely been considered un-patriotic to vote against it. It was however seen across both parties as a needed step in reaction to those attacks.

As one who lived through that time I can tell you that the U.S. was stunned during those events. The videos of the planes flying into the Twin-Towers of the World Trade Center were replayed 24X7 which is what we needed then. It was time for the President to act as commander-in-chief and go get those people who had done this to our country. Now these years after the fact many people feel that the Patriot Act was too much and cut through some liberties. At that time the people's liberty was assumed. What we needed then was a successful reaction from our government that would destroy those who tried to destroy us.

Five years later in 2006, Hillary would again vote to re-authorize the Patriot Act. But there was more in the Act at that time than there was in 2001. Some of those additions made the Act tighter and addressed issues specific as to the use of the Internet and the use of Wiretaps.

Additions to the act included:

Allows Internet service providers to disclose their subscriber's information and the contents of their communications to a government entity, if they believe there is "immediate danger of death or serious physical injury" (Sec. 107)

Requires that any court that allows a "roving wiretap" under the Foreign Intelligence Surveillance Act (FISA) must describe in great detail the intended target whose identity is not known (Sec. 108).

Clarifies that a convicted terrorist can be subject to the death penalty (Sec. 211).

The following is a list of some of the votes Hillary cast in her tenure as U.S. Senator for New York. I list only a small sampling of them here. There are far more but these represent her view on a few key issues in society today. If you want to review her entire voting record I highly recommend you visit VoteSmart.Org. It is a very full and complete website with of all the voting records as well as the content of the bills voted on in the House and Senate for many years. It is an unbiased website. It seeks only to inform its users of how their Representatives and Senators voted on the bills they wrote, co-sponsored, supported or rejected.

SELECTED HILLARY SENATE VOTES

GUNS AND GUN RIGHTS

Date   Bill No.   Bill Title

#1. 2-Mar-04 S 1805   Firearms Manufacturers Protection Bill did not Pass in the Senate   HILLARY VOTED NO

<u>Bill Overview:</u>

This was the first introduction of this bill in the Senate, it did not pass in 2004 but did pass in 2005. (See below) This was a very important bill to Gun Manufacturers. It prohibits civil lawsuits against manufacturers, dealers, and importers of firearms and ammunition. It prevents such groups from being sued due to criminal or unlawful use of their firearm products. Thereby it would have protected those manufacturers from being held legally responsible for anyone using their products in the commitment of a criminal act or act of terrorism. It also would have extended the federal assault weapons ban.

#2. 28-Jul-05 S Amdt 1626   Child Safety Lock Amendment This was adopted by the Senate   HILLARY VOTED YES

<u>Bill Overview:</u>

This was an amendment to an existing bill. It required all licensed importers, dealers and manufacturers of firearms to ensure their products are shipped and transferred in secure and safe packaging.

**#3. 29-Jul-05 S 397 Firearms Manufacturers Protection Bill
Bill was Passed in the Senate   HILLARY VOTED NO**

Bill Overview:

This was a bill similar to the earlier bill (S180) that failed a vote in the Senate in 2004.

This was the second introduction of this bill in the Senate.

Again this bill prohibits civil lawsuits against manufacturers, dealers, and importers of firearms and ammunition. It prevents such groups from being sued due to criminal or unlawful use of their firearm products. Hillary voted No for the second time.

TERRORISM

Date	Bill No.	Bill Title
#1. Oct. 25, 2001	**HR 3162**	**USA Patriot Act of**

**2001   Bill was Passed in the Senate   HILLARY
VOTED YES**

Bill Overview:

This was the original Patriot Act introduced by President George W. Bush after the September 11, 2001 Terrorist Attacks. It granted law enforcement organizations greater authority to search homes, track terrorist use of the Internet and perform landline based telephone wiretaps. It offered rewards to U.S. Citizens who helped the U.S. government identify and arrest terrorists. Allowed the Grand Jury to obtain and share information from law enforcement groups regarding those suspected as being terrorists. It allowed for greater government surveillance of suspected terrorists to investigate their financial networks, money laundering, and financial transactions that could be related to suspected terrorist activities.

#2. 2-Mar-06 HR 3199   PATRIOT Act Reauthorization
Conference Report was Adopted by the Senate
HILLARY VOTED YES

Bill Overview:

This was a conference report that amended the original Patriot Act. It extended the authority of the FBI to do "roving wiretaps" with access to business records through 2006 to December 31, 2009. It also made 14 provisions of the original Patriot Act permanent. It assigned three judges in the District of Columbia to hear petitions regarding improper requests from the FBI. Interestingly it allowed Internet Service providers to disclose subscriber's information and content information to a government entity if it was believed that there was "immediate danger of death or serious physical injury." It also included the provision that a terrorist can be subject to the death penalty.

#3. Sept. 28, 2006   S Amdt 5095
Oversight of CIA Interrogation and Detention Amendment
This Amendment was rejected by the Senate
HILLARY VOTED YES

Bill Overview:

Vote was to adopt an amendment that called for the Director of the CIA to report to Congress every three months. The Director would be required to provide a description of any detention facilities it utilized, the number of detainees, the interrogation techniques used and the intelligence gathered through those techniques. Called for the Inspector General of the CIA to provide an annual report detailing the CIA's adherence to U.S. laws regarding detention, interrogation and rendition programs. It also called for the Attorney General to report on the status of approved interrogation methods as being in compliance to the U.S. Constitution and any applicable treaties.

#4. Sept. 28, 2006 S 3930 Military Commissions Act of 2006 This Bill was Passed by the Senate   HILLARY VOTED NO

Bill Overview:

This bill created a military commission to try "enemy combatants" (non-soldiers) for violations of the laws of war. It also defined the rules and regulations for those commissions. An "unlawful enemy combatant," was defined as a non-US citizen who "purposefully and materially supported hostilities against the U.S. or its co-belligerents who is not a lawful enemy combatant (including a person who is part of the Taliban, al Qaeda, or associated forces)" and is not affiliated with any legal army, militia, or government organization. " It allowed the use as evidence in these proceedings of any related classified information but did not allow any such information to become public if it was detrimental to national security. Such evidence could also be obtained without a search warrant, etc. to be used in the trial of enemy combatants.

It defined the following crimes committed by an enemy combatant as "triable" by the military commission: rape, sexual assault or abuse, taking hostages, murder, spying, aiding the enemy, attacks on civilians and protected property, and terrorism. It prohibited statements obtained by torture from being used in an "enemy combatant" trial unless received prior to 2005. It allowed a judge to accept a confession if it was determined that the confession obtained was not through methods defined as "torture".

Lastly it prohibited an "enemy combatant" from invoking the Geneva Convention (for the treatment of soldiers in war-time) and invoking habeas corpus. Habeas Corpus is applicable to U.S. citizens. It is the legal submission to a court or tribunal petitioning it regarding unjustified incarceration or treatment.

#5. 19-Jul-07 S Amdt 2351   **Sense of the Senate on Guantanamo Bay Detainees**
This was Adopted by the Senate   HILLARY VOTED YES

Bill Overview:

This amendment expressed the "sense of the Senate" that any Guantanamo Bay detainees should not be released into the United States or transferred to prisons on U.S. soil. The goal was to prevent any transfer of such detainees to locations in the U.S. The primary reason for this was to not allow "enemy combatants" to be treated as a U.S. citizen under U.S. laws and courts and given Constitutional Rights only provided to U.S. citizens.

#6. 9-Jul-08   HR 6304   Foreign Intelligence Surveillance Act Amendments
This Bill Passed the Senate   HILLARY VOTED YES

Bill Overview:

This bill prohibited the targeting of U.S. citizens outside of the United States without approval of the foreign Intelligence Surveillance Court. It also prevents the targeting of such citizens with the intent of gaining information on a citizen located inside the United States. It limited the amount and kinds of surveillance that could be done to U.S. citizens inside and outside of the United States and its territories. It allowed providers of electronic communication to not be held liable due to their assistance to the government in surveillance activities within certain restrictions. Requires the Inspectors Generals of the DOJ, National Intelligence, NSA and DOD to submit a comprehensive report to Congress within one year of the passage of this bill.

Joseph V. McCauley

VARIOUS ISSUES

<u>Date</u>   <u>Bill No.</u>   <u>Bill Title</u>
#1. 25-Mar-04 HR 1997 Unborn Victims of Violence Act 2004
This Bill Passed the Senate   HILLARY VOTED NO

Bill Overview:

This bill would make it a criminal offense if a fetus/unborn child is injured or killed when someone is carrying out a violent crime on a pregnant woman.

Given Hillary's ardent pro-abortion stance her "No" vote is very in-line with the policies she and the Democratic Party have espoused for many years. It appears she is stating that an unborn child is not a person and therefore not eligible for legal protection.

#2. 6-Jun-07 S Amdt 1333   Barring Immigrants with Certain Criminal Histories Amendment
This was Adopted by the Senate HILLARY VOTED YES

Bill Overview:

This bill amendment would set up restrictions on admission to the U.S. for immigrants convicted of criminal behavior and penalties for illegal entry into the U.S. Penalties could range from six months to twenty years.

72

#3. 6-Jun-07   S Amdt 1250   Law Enforcement Review of Z Visa Application Amendment
This was Adopted by the Senate
HILLARY VOTED NO

Bill Overview:

This bill amendment allowed information contained in Z Visas (visas that have 3-year work permits and are renewable) to be made available to law enforcement given certain specified circumstances. The bill outlined what those circumstances are.

5 THE HILLARY SCANDALS LIST

The following is a list of the scandals that have come to light over the life and career of Hillary Clinton. Many of the alleged scandals have dogged and tarnished both Bill and Hillary's reputation over their thirty years in the public arena. If these scandals do anything they question the integrity of these two people to fill a high office like the Presidency.

"CATTLE FUTURES SCANDAL" - Hillary makes $100,000 profit on $1,000 investment in cattle futures contracts in 10 months. Investigations show possible questionable futures trading practices by Hillary or those representing her.

WHITE WATER SCANDAL- Hillary and Bill invest in the Whitewater Development Corp. That investment will eventually fail while raising questions about conflicts of interest, cronyism and possible illegal financial dealings.

"FILEGATE" scandal breaks in June 1996. Accusations alleged that the Director of the White House Office and Personnel Security received background report files on 700-900 people without authorization to do so. The files included records on previous Republican advisors and administration employees. An investigation held by later Impeachment prosecutor Kenneth Starr exonerates the Clintons due to lack of evidence. Final lawsuit by Judicial Watch ends in dismissal in 2010.

"TRAVELGATE" – Hillary fires seven employees of the White House Travel Office and replaces them with associates from Arkansas. Hillary has Billy Dale, head of the WHTO investigated by the FBI who was later found to have done nothing wrong but the investigation severely damaged his life and career.

WHITE WATER SCANDAL - After a two-year delay, records from the Whitewater Development Corporation that Bill and Hillary Clinton had invested in with Jim and Susan McDougal suddenly show up on a table in Hillary's "book room" at the White House. No one knowing how. Whitewater concerned possible conflict of interests, improper campaign contributions, political favors, and tax benefits on Hillary's part while acting as a lawyer at the Rose law firm.

PRESIDENT CLINTON LIES UNDER OATH - Bill Clinton already under investigation by Kenneth Starr sees that investigation expanded into impeachment proceedings due to Clinton lying under oath about his extramarital affair with Monica Lewinsky. Hillary calls the allegations part of a "vast right-wing conspiracy". Later Bill admits to Hillary that the affair did take place. Was Hillary involved in Bill's strategy?

PRESIDENT CLINTON IS IMPEACHED- President Clinton is impeached by the House of Representatives.

SNIPER FIRE STORY - Hillary's statements about being under-fire by snipers in a 1996 visit to Bosnia were proved as not true and drew heavy media attention. The videos of the arrival show no sniper fire.

BENGHAZI - Just two months prior to the 2012 U.S. Presidential elections on September 11, terrorists invade the U.S. diplomatic facility in Benghazi, Libya. Benghazi is not the U.S. embassy but a second U.S. location in Libya. However the U.S. Ambassador is there at the time. He and three others are killed and a total of two U.S. diplomatic locations have buildings set on fire. Ambassador Christopher Stevens is the first U.S. Ambassador killed in the line of duty since 1979.

The scandal that comes out of the attack is what appears to be a deliberate attempt by Hillary Clinton and President Obama to persuade the American Public that the attacks were based on a "spontaneous" riot reaction to an anti-Muslim video called "Innocence of Muslims". On-going investigations reveal that the attacks were planned in advance to be carried out on the anniversary of the September 11, 2001 attacks. Congressional investigations into Benghazi continue into 2016.

.

BENGHAZI - January 23, 2013 Hillary testifies to the Benghazi Congressional Committee regarding the 9/11/2012 attacks in Benghazi. Continued new information that comes to light shows that original reports on the attack we edited or changed to blame the attack on spontaneous riots due to an anti-Muslim video. It appears she lied.

"EMAIL GATE" - March 2015, Just prior to her announcing her second Presidential bid Hillary made public the fact that she had used a private email server while Secretary of State instead of the normal secure in-house Dept. of State email services. She noted that she had deleted 30,000 private emails and that at no time had she received or sent secret or classified emails through that server. This came to light due to the fact that the Special Committee on Benghazi had subpoenaed her emails for the investigation the committee was doing regarding the Benghazi incident.

"EMAIL GATE" - By October 2015 an independent FBI investigation was underway to ascertain if Clinton as Secretary of State had mishandled secret or classified U. S information.   By October the FBI had retrieved several thousands of emails that Hillary had "wiped" from the server. As of January 2016 some 1,300 emails have been restored by the FBI that had been identified as classified, secret, or top secret by their original senders.

BENGHAZI - On October 22, 2015 Hillary testifies for 11 hours before the Congressional Committee on the Libyan attacks of 9/11/2012. Her emails released immediately after the hearing show that Hillary did acknowledge that the Benghazi attack was perpetrated by an "Al-Quida like group" as she states in the emails. It was not the work of a spontaneous riot due to an anti Muslim video.

"SON-IN-LAW GATE" – 2015 - a legal watch group called FACT (Foundation for Accountability and Civic Trust) calls for a federal probe to see if Secretary Clinton gave special treatment to a mining company due to her son-in-law's relationship with that company.

CLINTON FOUNDATATION – various groups have called for a probe into the donors of the Clinton Foundation and their possible influence on Hillary's tenure as Secretary of State. This is due to their large contributions made to the Clinton Foundation during that time. Possible conflicts of interests have come up in various State Department released emails. They show links to high-paid speaking engagements for Bill Clinton from countries possibly seeking favors from Hillary's during her 2009-2013 time at the Department of State.

"EMAIL GATE" - By mid-January 2016 it was found that several dozens of classified, secret, top secret and ultra-secret (SAP or Special Access Program) State Department Emails were on Hillary's unsecure Email server.

This list is incomplete as there are many other alleged questionable practices that have arisen from the careers of a young Governor from Arkansas and a young woman lawyer from Illinois. Yes, there are conspiracy theorists coming out of the woodwork searching for more Clinton scandals. Will more be found? Well, no one expected her Department of State email situation to come up and it did. Hillary dismissed it as a wrong judgment call on her part. Yet she was careful to delete 30,000 emails before she revealed what had happened. Now, after the fact, there is an investigation to confirm or deny if classified materials were mishandled by Hillary or her staff. If history is any indicator it would seem a foregone conclusion that more "scandals" will arise. The ones listed here are the ones that are the currently best well known and with an established trail of witnesses and documentation of their own.

Does not this list, in and of it self, beg the question "what is going on here?" Why does America have to deal with these kinds of situations again and again? If a person has integrity then they act with integrity and scenarios like these should not be even be coming up. If either Bill or Hillary are never convicted for anything the list of allegations was, is, and continues to be sadly alarming and concerning.

Should Hillary be considered trustworthy enough to President? Hillary's history would imply, " I don't think so."

Could we assume she would be honest with the American public if she was President?

Hillary's history says "No".

6 HILLARY AS U.S. SECRETARY OF STATE

Now we come to one of the most debated periods of the political career of Hillary Clinton. Hillary was the U.S. Secretary of State from January 2009 to February of 2013. President-elect Obama offered Hillary this role soon after the election of 2008. By her own admission she rejected it and felt others could do the job. Obama persisted and she eventually accepted his offer. It is clear however that Hillary went for the Secretary of State role as a resume' enhancer for the next rung of the ladder to the Presidency. It worked for Thomas Jefferson why not her? By serving in that role she would be able to position herself as skilled in foreign policy. Lack of foreign policy experience has been a political short fall that has dogged many a presidential candidate including her boss, Barak Obama. He, as a junior U.S. senator with minimal legislation or voting record in the Senate, carried a lack of foreign policy credentials as a major political deficit for him going into the 2008 election cycle.

Hillary's recommendations as Secretary were in some cases overruled by what appeared to be Obama's pro-Muslim leanings. For example she and the President disagreed about retaining U.S. troops in Iraq after the planned pull out date. The end result however of the final choices of the Clinton-Obama foreign policy would leave the world scene a far less secure and peaceful place. Let me point out again that Hillary did vote for the War in Iraq while serving as a Senator. However she would later condemn that vote. She blamed mis-information from the Bush Administration that painted the wrong picture of Iraq so as to justify Bush launching the war there.

Was that political flip-flopping to position herself better within the Democratic Party?

Certainly a strong possibility given Hillary's past.

Here is how Hillary would sum up her foreign policy goals as the Secretary of State. I quote from her first speech to the State Department where she said:

"There are three legs to the stool of American foreign policy: defense, diplomacy, and development. And we are responsible for two of the three legs. And we will make clear, as we go forward, that diplomacy and development are essential tools in achieving the long-term objectives of the United States. And I will do all that I can, working with you, to make it abundantly clear that robust diplomacy and effective development are the best long-term tools for securing America's future."

The world was her operating theater, but the Middle East would prove to be the particularly troublesome diplomatic area that would become the focal point of her time in office. Specifically this would include Iraq, Libya, Iran, Syria, and Afghanistan.

The Middle East that was in place after President George W. Bush was one in which America had brought freedom to some 56 million citizens of Afghanistan and Iraq. Women and young girls living in Iraq and Afghanistan now had more opportunities to go to school and better their lives. Generally there was a real appreciation from the citizens of those countries for what America had done for them.

People there had voted in national elections for the first time ever. They did so often overcoming opposition and death threats from the terrorist elements of Islam. I can recall the videos of men and women in Iraq holding up index fingers that had been dipped in a purple dye, indicating they had successfully voted. It was a proud moment for them and for America. Under President Bush the U.S. had ended the threat that came from Usama Bin Laden out of Afghanistan, had toppled the Taliban, and removed Saddam Hussein as dictator of Iraq.

Since leaving the Secretary post Hillary has been working from 2014 on to position herself as successful in the foreign policy actions she took while in office. However she continues to be confronted by the attacks in Benghazi in 2012 and the false statements she made about them. Looking at the historical record we could say that Hillary is not to be blamed for all of the final policy decisions and actions taken by Obama after she left the Secretary post. What grew out of the mistakes of her policies at the Department of State has become the failure of the Obama Administration to deal successfully with ISIS and global Islamist terrorism. As Secretary of State any person serving in that capacity can be overruled by the President. In the end the ultimate policy call is the President's and what he implements is his responsibility. But let's start at the beginning by looking at how her boss began his rollout of his foreign policy in his first term.

OBAMA'S "APOLOGY" TOUR

Obama began what has been chidingly called his "apology tour" of U.S. allies in his first term. He infuriated many Americans by his attitude and actions toward the heads of state he encountered on that tour. Most famously was his deep waisted bow when greeting King

Abdullah of Saudi Arabia on April 1, 2009. (Happy April Fool's Day!) This tour was his first foreign policy act less than four full months into his first term. He followed that with a bow to Queen Elizabeth of Great Britain and the Emperor of Japan. Most Americans found this series of acts demeaning to U.S. exceptionalism and position on the world stage. We were, and are, the leading superpower in the world. The bow to King Abdullah was particularly distasteful in that it appeared that the President of the United States was showing subservience to that King. It looked like the puppy dog that rolls over on its back in submission to the "big" dog. It was not appreciated.

Obama introduced a new era in U.S. Foreign Policy. His desire was to "make up" for what he interpreted as the mistakes of the Bush Administration and American "imperialist" foreign policy of prior administrations generally. He opposed the war in Iraq and ran on the platform that he would remove troops from that country as soon as possible. If the Obama foreign policy has seemed confused it is mostly the outcome of his inexperience and amateur-like approach to that segment of his presidency. After all he did choose a person with no prior international foreign policy experience as his Secretary of State- Hillary Clinton. Both were starting from scratch beginning their new roles with no practical background in foreign affairs and diplomacy.

2009

As Secretary Hillary did support the increase of 21,000 troops in Afghanistan, which was the recommendation of the generals working on the battlefield. This increase was called "the Surge" which was a similar strategy used by George W. Bush for Iraq in 2007. This position was supported by many Republicans and Conservatives at the time. This was in March of 2009. The Pentagon had determined that more troops were needed on the ground to defeat the Taliban. Obama sent the additional troops to the battlefield while still wanting to set a timeline for the ultimate withdrawal. But the war had to be won first. The increase in ground troops worked. It was the military strategy that was needed at that time. In this particular case Hillary made the right decision to support the "Surge" in Afghanistan in spite of her change of mind about the War in Iraq. She was criticized for her support of this move at the time and continues to be so by her Democratic Presidential rivals. In fact in some instances Hillary can be viewed as being more "hawkish" than her boss, Barak Obama.

RUSSIA

In March of 2009 Hillary went to meet with the Russian Foreign Minister at the time, Sergey Lavrov to start a new relationship with Russia. She did this through a hokey "Reset Button" she presented to Lavrov in a short ceremony. It was a well-intentioned gesture but unfortunately it reflected the amateurish and ill thought out foreign policy of the Obama-Clinton administration. That policy would be on disappointing display in the coming years of Hillary's tenure as Secretary of State. The "Reset" button was supposed to have the Russian word for "reset" on it much like the famous Staple's "Easy" button. Unfortunately THE United States State Department could not get the Russian translation right and instead of "Reset" the button read "Overcharged." It proved one of the more embarrassing points of the early days of the Clinton Secretary time in office.

IRAQ

President Obama's approach to Iraq has been driven more by ideology rather than the practicality of the need of the times. It was compounded by his failure to not follow the advice of his military advisers. The Pentagon was united in its recommendation that Obama not remove all troops from Iraq at once as he had promised as part of his Presidential campaign. Hillary as it later came out was for keeping some level of U.S. troops in Iraq using what is known as a "Status of Forces Agreement." Such an agreement would allow U.S. troops to remain for some period of time and the SOFA would define the mission of those troops as they remained in Iraq.

In reference to this here is what was said in an article by Josh Rogin from his interview with Hillary in 2014. It was reported on "The Daily Beast", an American news reporting and opinion website. The article has two specific comments about Hillary's role as Secretary of State during the negotiations for the pull out of U.S. forces from Iraq:

"Hillary Clinton was a lion for keeping troops there," James Jeffrey, who was the U.S. ambassador to Iraq in 2011, told The Daily Beast in an interview. "She was a strong advocate for keeping troops there past 2011," when American forces eventually withdrew.

Clinton placed the blame for the failure of the negotiations on Maliki (Prime Minister of Iraq from 2006 to 2014) She said the administration had offered him a Status of Forces Agreement with American troops attached, but he didn't accept.

Ali Khedery in the Washington Post of July 3, 2014 adds to this perspective in a very insightful and interesting article. The article paints an intriguing history of what brought the now ex-Prime Minister of Iraq, Nouri al-Maliki, into and then out of power. Ali Khedery is chairman and chief executive of the Dubai-based Dragoman Partners. From 2003 to 2009, he was the longest continuously serving American official in Iraq, acting as a special assistant to five U.S. ambassadors and as a senior adviser to three heads of U.S. Central Command. In 2011, as an executive with Exxon Mobil, he negotiated the company's entry into the Kurdistan Region of Iraq.

Once Prime Minister Maliki took power he began to remove his political rivals. As a Shiite, he detested the Sunni-minority rule of Iraq. Once in place, starting in 2006 through the last two years of the Bush Presidency, Maliki consolidated power and put Iraq on the path that would eventually lead to the dismemberment of that country and the sweeping advance over it by ISIS in 2014-2015. In 2008 Maliki began using the Iraq Army against his political rivals. Overall his leadership was sectarian and divisive with Sunni and Kurdish leaders accusing him for his consolidation of power. The picture painted in the article shows an Obama-Clinton Administration that failed to see the warning signs of what was happening in Iraq as the nation turned away from Maliki. Eventually ISIS would rise to power taking over major parts of that country. Obama, for all his disdain for what George W. Bush did in his invasion of Iraq (Bush's "dumb war") seriously dropped the ball and that ultimately led to the ISIS atrocities of the present day.

Vice President Biden visited Iraq in September of 2010. In spite of opposing and contrary counsel at multiple levels he saw Prime Minister Maliki as the only workable political leader for Iraq. He felt that Maliki would accept the Status of Forces agreement even stating, *"I'll bet you my vice presidency Maliki will extend the SOFA," referring to the status-of-forces agreement that would allow U.S. troops to remain in Iraq past 2011."*

Maliki did not.

Uncle Joe Biden is still Vice President.

So in Iraq the U.S. had to deal with a leader it had set up and whose policies would lead to the tearing apart of what the U.S. had very significantly achieved in the Iraq War. This would be compounded and finalized by a series of wrong choices of the Obama-Clinton administration. As is stated in the Ali Khedery article,

"By November (2010), the White House had settled on its disastrous Iraq strategy. The Iraqi constitutional process and election results would be ignored, and America would throw its full support behind Maliki."

The advance of ISIS should rest squarely on the shoulders of Hillary Clinton and Barak Obama. It started under Hillary's term as Secretary of State. After Hillary's departure from the Department it was Obama's continuing signature failure that he did not act to address the increasingly dangerous rising tide of ISIS. That tide has led to the displacement of millions of people, many who are now refugees from Syria. We can add to that the death of the estimated thousands of Christians and Muslims at the hands of ISIS and their known enslavement of women and girls as sex slaves. This barbarity has included the destruction of several historically important archeological sites that ISIS deemed offensive to Islam. What Obama mistakenly called the "JV Team" has now become a terrorist powerhouse that the world has to reckon with. It should be noted that Hillary never came out publically in opposition to Obama's "JV" definition of the threat of ISIS.

ISIS AND SYRIA

ISIS has now become the most significant terrorist organization of modern times. The start to all of this was when Obama failed to follow the counsel of his senior military leader-ship to leave a residual force behind in Iraq when the U.S. left in 2011. Obama choose rather to fulfill his campaign pledge to pull all troops out of that country instead of doing what has now turned out to have been the more prudent and correct strategy.

Here is a short history of the actions that led to the dismemberment of Iraq, Syria, and the rise of ISIS:

- Syria has had a 5-year Civil War. The Dictator of that country Bashar al-Assad has been fighting against reforms since he took over from his father, Hafaez al-Assad who died in 2000.

- March 2011 – Assad fires on peaceful Arab Spring demonstrators.

- July 2011 – The demonstrator's decide to fire back resulting in that some Syrian soldiers defect from the Syrian army.

o Those soldiers become the Free Syrian Army.

o Assad allows Muslim extremists into Syria. He also releases some Islamic radicals from Syrian prisons to taint the Free Syrian Army movement as radicals.

- January 2012 – Al Qaida forms a new branch in Syria.
    - o Syrian Kurdish groups secede from Syrian rule and a proxy war begins.
    - o Iran intercedes for Assad and sends daily cargo flights and people to help Assad.
    - o Oil rich Arab states send money to the Rebels via Turkey to resist the influence of Iran.
    - o Hezbollah – a group backed by Iran invades Syria to fight with Assad.
    - o Saudi Arabia starts going through Jordan to send more money to the Rebels.

- August 2012 - President Obama was asked what he would do if Syria began using weapons of mass destruction, specifically poison gas, on its citizens.

The question to the President was this:

"Mr. President, could you update us on your latest thinking of where you think things are in Syria, and in particular, whether you envision using U.S. military, if simply for nothing else, the safe keeping of the chemical weapons, and if you're confident that the chemical weapons are safe?"

President Obama's answer included this statement:

"I have, at this point, not ordered military engagement in the situation. But the point that you made about chemical and biological weapons is critical. That's an issue that doesn't just concern Syria; it concerns our close allies in the region, including Israel. It concerns us. We cannot have a situation where chemical or biological weapons are falling into the hands of the wrong people.

"We have been very clear to the Assad regime, but also to other players on the ground, that a red line for us is when we start seeing a whole bunch of chemical weapons moving around or being utilized. That would change my calculus. That would change my equation."

- 2013 – Sunnis Muslims gather to oppose Assad, Shiites gather to support Assad.

  - April- 2013 Obama Administration sends a secret order to the CIA to train and equip Syrian rebels.
  - The United States asks various gulf-states to stop supporting extremists. They decline.
  - Assad uses chemical weapons against his own people.

President Obama when confronted with the "red-line" statement he made earlier in which he said he would act should Assad use chemical weapons, does nothing. Instead through his Press Secretary he back peddles saying that it was "the world's red line". He still does nothing and looks like a fool who talks tough, but cannot follow through.

  - Assad's Syria gets continued support from Russia
  - U.S. trained rebels join the anti-Assad fighters and the U.S. is now participating in the Syrian Civil War.

- 2014- ISIS breaks away from Al Qaida and creates the Islamic State of Iraq and Syria.
  - ISIS becomes Al Qaida's enemy and does not fight Assad. It fights the Rebels and the Kurds.

  - ISIS sets up its Caliphate across Iraq and parts of Syria taking major Syrian cities under its control.

  - August 2014 – Turkey begins bombing Kurdish forces on the ground.

  - Turkey does not bomb ISIS in Syria.

o Kurds are confused about where the USA stands towards them.

o Assad continues to lose control as ISIS captures large parts of Syria and Iraq.

o Sept 2014 – Obama says he will begin bombing ISIS.

o USA begins another training program of the Rebels but only those who will fight ISIS. The program fails.

o The failed program shows America opposes ISIS more than Assad.

- Sept 2015 – Russia begins bombing U.S. allies in Syria on the pretense it is actually bombing ISIS.

- October 2015- ISIS claims responsibility for a bomb on a Russian civilian aircraft flying from Egypt to Russia killing all on board. Russia actually starts bombing ISIS positions.

- November 2015 – ISIS claims responsibility for a Paris Terrorist cell that kills 130 and wounds a total of 500 people at a concert hall and restaurants in Paris France on Friday, November 13. The French government retaliates with several hundred raids on suspected terrorist cells. Belgium follows suit after links to the Paris attack are found in Brussels. France begins bombing ISIS.

- December 2015 – a Muslim husband and wife couple radicalized in the U.S. open fire on a Christmas Party at the Regional Inland Center in San Bernardino, Ca., attacking the group where the husband was employed. He had attended the party earlier, left and came back with his wife armed with semiautomatic weapons and pipe bombs. They opened fire and fled. Very quick police work finds the couple en-route from their house surrounds and kills them in a firefight. It is the worst U.S. terrorist attack since 9/11. Obama calls for more gun control. Instead of making a trip to California to specifically address the terrorist attack as George W. Bush did after 9/11, Obama stops in California for a very un-inspiring visit with the relatives of the victims. He then leaves for his Christmas vacation in Hawaii.

American leadership regarding terrorism is nowhere to be found and uncertainty reigns. Americans question what if anything Obama is really doing to keep the people of the U.S. safe.

IRAN

Hillary, according to the sources I reviewed for this book, was successful in pulling together the nations that would implement UN based sanctions against Iran. If true then that is to her credit. This would include Russia and China, who are strange bedfellows not known for cooperating with the West as well as between themselves. Those sanctions were credited as the primary drivers that impacted the Iranian economy and drove the Iranian government to the bargaining table after Hillary left the State Department in 2013.

AFTER HILLARY – JOHN KERRY

Eventually in 2014 and into 2015 the new Secretary of State, John Kerry and President Obama would negotiate a nuclear deal with Iran. The goal was to prevent Iran from developing a nuclear bomb. That deal has been decried and discredited by many government leaders across the globe. It was perceived as giving Iran everything it wanted without the real safeguards and inspections needed to ensure Iran's compliance. The American public has also looked at this deal with great skepticism. They consider it as one of the failed attempts of the Obama Administration to effectively address Jihadist terrorism. Iran is considered a sponsor of world terrorism due to its long standing support of terrorism and its current displays of strong anti-U.S. and anti-Israel sentiment at large public demonstrations held there.

LYBIA

Hillary's and Obama's handling of Libya is seen as another major foreign policy failure. Even though Muammar Gaddafi was a dictator he was not as of 2011 an active enemy of the U.S. Since assuming the leadership of Libya in 1969 Kaddafi began financing Muslim extremism in order to work against Arab leaders he opposed. Initially friendly with Anwar Sadat, the President of Egypt, their relationship deteriorated precipitously after Sadat signed a peace accord with Israel. Previously Gaddafi was furious that Sadat had not included him on the planning for what would later be called the Yom Kippur War with Israel.

Over time Gaddafi's influence would spread to the Sudan when he sponsored the Sudanese People's Liberation Army to overthrow Sudanese President Gaafar Nimiery. He would also sponsor anti-government rebels in Tunisia and Morocco. He implemented strong socialist control of Libya throughout the 1970s eliminating private enterprise and creating a central government that controlled the economy. Libya has been on the U.S. State Department's list of "State Sponsors of Terrorism" since 1979. Gaddafi was a terrorist at heart and funded the spread of it against those who either offended him or opposed his policies. Many viewed him, including the Soviet Union in the 1980s, as unpredictable, crazy, and dangerous.

By the time 2011 arrived Libya was on the brink of Civil War. Large-scale protests broke out against Gaddafi in February of 2011. Gaddafi responded by killing protestors starting in Benghazi, killing hundreds. This then expanded into a full-scale civil war. By March 2011 NATO was involved and declared a no fly zone to defend the civilian population from attacks from the air by Gaddafi's air force. Eventually an air attack by NATO on April 30th would kill Gaddafi's sixth son and three of his grandsons. Amnesty International would then charge Gaddafi with "crimes against humanity". He would finally be captured by a group of anti-Gaddafi militia and was brutally murdered on October 20, 2011.

In order to facilitate regime change and remove Gaddafi the U.S. under the Obama-Clinton foreign policy joined with the NATO intervention and bombed the Libyan army. The team of Obama-Clinton were OK with removing Gaddafi but failed to act in the more strategically important country of Syria after Assad used chemical weapons on his own people. If American political leadership had been exercised in Syria in 2012-2013 it may very well have prevented the creation of the ISIS terrorist threat that we see today.

BENGHAZI

Finally Libya provides the last and one of the more important failures of the Clinton Foreign Policy. This was the attack on the American diplomatic compound in Benghazi on September 11, 2012. This would be a major stain on Hillary's role as Secretary of State. The official story that unfolded after the attacks in Benghazi has proved to be filled with mis-representations of the facts given by the President, Hillary, and the American UN ambassador, Susan Rice. It marked a high level of political deceitfulness that further darkened Hillary's image and that of Barak Obama.

The major issues regarding the attack are these:

1. What was the cause of the attacks?
2. Why wasn't additional security provided after repeated requests by the U.S. Ambassador.
3. Why wasn't available U.S. military assistance sent to defend against the attacks?
4. Why did Hillary's State Department and Obama lie about the root cause of the attacks?

Within days of the attacks that killed the U.S. Ambassador and three other Americans, the UN Ambassador Susan Rice was on the Sunday talk shows. She stated that the cause of the attacks was a spontaneous Muslim reaction to a vulgar and ardently anti-Muslim video about Mohammed posted to the Internet. What has been in question since then is who created the talking points, blaming the video and not terrorism? There appears to have been a planned and deliberate effort by Hillary, Obama, and Rice to not give the correct information to the American public. Secondly there was the question as to why U.S. military forces that could have gone in to assist were held back and never sent. That series of events on 9/11/2012 launched a Congressional Hearing on Benghazi that has continued to this day.

The hearings have seen major stonewalling from the State Department in providing subpoenaed emails and other documentation that would shed light on what were the events of that night. Hillary, Susan Rice, and then Obama would continue to blame the attacks on the Internet video. They decried it as something the U.S. government would never support or do, so as to not insult Muslims. They would tell this story as the bodies of the American heroes were returned to the United States. At the ceremony on their return Hillary was still sticking to that Internet video story including it in her comments made at the time.

The reasons for the delay in not sending U.S. forces to help defend the compound are still in limbo. It appears that the forces needed were ready and could have been sent. They were however told to stand down and not transport to the compound to provide assistance. Former Secretary of the Defense, Leon Panetta stated that there was not sufficient time to get the military support there in time to really help. That was not the case since no one knew when the attacks would end. In fact, there ended up being three different "waves" of attacks that went into the early dawn of the next day. The at-ready military assets and personnel could have been sent anyway. Accusations continue to fly both ways and with a great deal of finger pointing as who is to blame. Does Hillary deserve some blame? Perhaps or perhaps not in regards to the delay in holding off the troops that could have been sent to help. She does however carry responsibility for not acting on numerous requests from Ambassador Christopher Stevens asking for more security personnel in Libya. Apparently there were many emails to that effect sent to Hillary personally. No action was ever taken.

Fast forward to October through November of 2015. It has now been proven that Hillary privately assessed that the Benghazi attack was in fact a terrorist one. Through a lawsuit filed by Judicial Watch, a government watchdog organization, a series of emails came to light regarding that sad night in 2012. The emails show Hillary emailing her daughter, Chelsea, what she (Hillary) defined as the real cause of the attacks. The emails were sent to "Diane Reynolds" the alias Hillary used in her email for Chelsea. The email reads:

"From: H

Sent: Tuesday, September 11, 2012 11:11 PM

To: Diane Reynolds

Subject: Re: I'm in my office

Two of our officers were killed in Benghazi by an Al Qaeda-like group. The Ambassador, whom I handpicked and a young communications officer on temporary duty with a wife and two young children. Very hard day and I fear more of the same tomorrow."

In a statement given after this email she issued an official State Department press release blaming the attack on the Internet video. It is clear that Hillary knew what she was doing in the issuing of the public statement blaming the Internet video. In her email to Chelsea she defined the attacks as done by "an Al-Qaeda like group", a long-standing terrorist organization. There was absolutely no justification to blame the video. No statement was ever made by the attackers confirming the video as the cause of the attacks. The attackers were too well armed and prepared for this to have been spontaneous. They knew exactly where they were going in that compound and when.

Now the reason for the façade, the lying about what really happened?

To get Barak Obama re-elected.

The 2012 Presidential elections were only two months after the attacks. The actions Hillary, Obama, and Ambassador Rice took were just damage control against President Obama's previous claim that Al-Qaeda was contained and no longer a viable threat.

Hillary has now testified twice in front of the Congressional Committee on Benghazi. In both testimonies some statements she made have been proven questionable or false in the light of later email releases from the State Department.

DEPARTMENT OF STATE EMAIL SCANDAL

The cloud of suspicion once again arose over Hillary when in March of 2015 she let the world know that she had used a private email server while acting as U.S. Secretary of State. She had deleted some 30,000 emails that she said were private in nature and did not involve State Department business. She claimed that no emails she received on that private server were classified, secret, or top secret and that at no time were such kinds of emails sent through her server. She also claimed that she had surrendered all required emails. It was as if she was saying, 'now it was time to go run for the Presidency and the U.S. public should forget about the emails.'

Well not so fast.

In October of 2015 it turned out that Clinton confidant Sidney Blumenthal had kept a large number of emails from Hillary in her duties as Secretary that he had retained on a portable thumb drive. Blumenthal did not have any of the security clearances required by the State Department when he received them. He turned the emails over to Congress as was requested by the Benghazi hearings. Hillary also hadn't surrendered personal emails she had sent to General David Petraeus during her time at State.

Embarrassingly for the State Department one of Hillary's aids at State, Huma Abedin, had woefully complained to Hillary in an email about the poor technical capabilities of the State Department's email system. She stated: "*NO ONE uses a State-issued laptop and even high officials routinely end up using their home email accounts to be able to get their work done quickly.*" Mrs. Clinton—from her private email—agreed that, "*it is a problem.*" Even if that was the case Hillary had the legal responsibility and, it is assumed the diplomatic understanding, to identify and safeguard confidential Department of State information. To not keep safe U.S. State Department confidential and secret materials or, to allow unauthorized persons access to national defense information, could be a violation of the U.S. Espionage Act of 1913.

As to the claim that there were no classified emails on Hillary's server? In October 2015 the FBI (in its own independent investigation) had found more that 400 emails from Hillary's private server that contained classified information. In that group of released Emails from the State Department was one where Hillary instructed an aide on her staff to send sensitive information without the appropriate classification i.e. with the "confidential, secret, or top secret" heading removed. That is a federal offense. Additionally the server Hillary used during her time at State was located in an unsecure building, not a secure data center. To make matters worse it was disclosed in October of 2015 that Hillary's server was attacked at least five times by hackers associated with Russia.

Later, as of January 2016 over 1,300 classified emails have been found. In mid-January 2016 the Inspector General assigned to the U.S. Intelligence Community in a letter to a Senate Sub-Committee let it be known that several dozens of Secret, Top-Secret, and ultra-secret (SAP or Special Access Program) emails were found on Hillary's server.

The email scandal will continue being discussed for a long time. Since she is being investigated by the FBI the question comes up as to what happens if Hillary is indicted before the 2016 Elections? And what if she is convicted? Can she run for and then be President? The answer is: it's debatable. There is nothing in the Constitutional requirement for a U.S. President that states that someone under indictment or a convicted felon cannot run for or be elected President. It is debatable if a President can indeed pardon him or herself. The opinions of most constitutional scholars however state that such an act would be unconstitutional. If someone in the House of Representatives is convicted of a felony they go to prison and lose their seat. Impeachment is the only Congressional tool available to remove a President for "high crimes and misdemeanors." Lastly, President Obama could pardon her even before her being indicted or convicted leaving her free to run. A President can pardon anyone before or after an indictment and even prior to being convicted.

President Gerald Ford pardoned Richard Nixon after Nixon had resigned. Nixon however had no pending indictment facing him. Ford simply pardoned him causing a political firestorm after doing so. Ford's justification for the pardon was that it was in the best interest of the country and that for the Nixon family this **"is a tragedy in which we all have played a part. It could go on and on and on, or someone must write the end to it. I have concluded that only I can do that, and if I can, I must**." Obama could use the same justification or others to pardon Hillary. Interestingly President Ford's granting of the pardon may have cost him the election in 1976.

Where will all the events of Hillary's history play out in the days ahead? It remains to be seen.

It is clear the Clinton-Obama foreign policy has left its impact on the world. The results? Iraq is in splinters, the ascendancy of ISIS, no resolution to Syria, millions of refugees with probable embedded terrorists going to Europe and America, Libya open to Islamic extremism, no real reset with Russia, the alienation of Arab allies, and Israel–American relations in their worst condition in fifty years. Surely all this does raise this question.

Should Hillary Clinton as one of the main architects of this failed foreign policy be President?

I think not.

7 THE FUTURE

If you started reading this book as a supporter of Hillary Clinton I hope what you have seen here has given you an alternative view. I cannot support her in her run for President. I could not in 2008 and will not in 2016.

Who do I blame for that?

I blame Hillary.

This book outlines why.

Right now our country desperately needs a real leader. We need a Lincoln, a Theodore Roosevelt, a Reagan, or a George Washington, and yes, a Margaret Thatcher.

Hillary is no Margaret Thatcher.

We need a leader who will inspire us while developing this country's needed solutions for the short and long-term and then successfully implement them. We need a leader who will be honest with the American people and has proven him or herself worthy of our trust.

We need someone to make us proud to be Americans. Again.

You decide!

SOURCES USED IN THIS BOOK:

Hillary Clinton

http://history.howstuffworks.com/historical-figures/hillary-clinton2.html https://www.whitehouse.gov/1600/first-ladies/hillary_clinton

http://www.history.com/topics/firstladies/hillary rodham-clinton

http://www.pbs.org/wgbh/americanexperience/features/biography/clinton-hillary/

https://www.hillaryclinton.com/about/bio/

https://en.wikipedia.org/wiki/Hillary_Clinton

What Is Hillary's Greatest Accomplishment?
http://www.politico.com/magazine/story/2015/09/carly-fiorina-debate-hillary-clintons-greatest-accomplishment-213157

Hillary Clinton
http://rationalwiki.org/wiki/Hillary_Clinton

Hillary Clinton Biography
http://www.biography.com/people/hillary-clinton-9251306

https://www.govtrack.us/

http://www.washingtontimes.com/news/2015/aug/23/madison-gesiotto-potential-obama-pardoning-hillary/

President Obama's Red Line
https://www.washingtonpost.com/news/fact checker/wp/2013/09/06/president-obama-and-the-red-line-on-syrias-chemical-weapons/

Hillary as Secretary of State
https://en.wikipedia.org/wiki/Hillary_Rodham_Clinton%27s_tenure_as_Secretary_of_State

Why We Stuck with Maliki and Lost Iraq
https://www.washingtonpost.com/opinions/why-we-stuck-with-maliki--and-lost-iraq/2014/07/03/0dd6a8a4-f7ec-11e3-a606-946fd632f9f1_story.html

The Atlantic – Failure to Help Syrian Rebels Led to the Rise of ISIS
http://www.theatlantic.com/international/archive/2014/08/hillary-clinton-failure-to-help-syrian-rebels-led-to-the-rise-of-isis/375832/

Hillary Clinton Pushed Obama to Keep Troops in Iraq
http://www.thedailybeast.com/articles/2014/06/18/hillary-clinton-pushed-obama-to-keep-troops-in-iraq.html

Hillary Clinton's $13M fail as Secretary of State
http://nypost.com/2016/01/01/hillary-clintons-13m-fail-as-secretary-of-state/

Was Hillary Clinton a Good Secretary of State?
https://www.washingtonpost.com/opinions/was-hillary-clinton-a-good-secretary-of-state/2014/05/30/16daf9c0-e5d4-11e3-a86b-362fd5443d19_story.html

Bombshell: In Email, Hillary Ordered Aide to Strip Classified Marking and Send Sensitive Material
http://townhall.com/tipsheet/guybenson/2016/01/08/boom-in-newlyreleased-email-hillary-orders-aide-to-strip-classified-marking-n2101680

Evidence may be mounting that Democratic presidential candidate Hillary Clinton violated a provision in the federal Espionage Act.
http://www.breitbart.com/big-government/2015/10/16/gross-negligence-report-suggests-hillary-clinton-violated-espionage-act/

Alleged Hillary Scandals
A Hillary Clinton Email Scandal Checklist
http://www.wsj.com/articles/a-clinton-email-scandal-checklist-1443739607

BREAKING: Newly Discovered Letters Between Hillary Clinton & Saul Alinsky (Marxist & Community Organizer)
http://www.thepoliticalinsider.com/breaking-newly-discovered-letters-hillary-clinton-saul-alinsky-marxist-community-organizer/#ixzz3tMivi2bu

Hillary Rodham senior thesis
https://en.wikipedia.org/wiki/Hillary_Rodham_senior_thesis

Hillary Clinton Campaign Scandals – They've become Exhausting
http://www.nationalreview.com/article/423462/hillarys-campaign

10 Scandals Involving Hillary Clinton You May Have Forgotten
http://www.mrctv.org/blog/10-scandals-involving-hillary-clinton-you-may-have-forgotten#.0ao38jm:6iKY

Washingtonpost.com: Whitewater Time Line
http://www.washingtonpost.com/wpsrv/politics/special/whitewatertimeline.

From Whitewater to Benghazi: A Clinton Scandal Primer
http://www.theatlantic.com/politics/archive/2015/10/tracking-theClinton Scandals

The Top 17 Hillary Clinton Scandals http://presidential-candidates.insidegov.com/stories/5955/top-hillary-clinton-scandals#Intro

Hillary Clinton says religious beliefs 'have to be changed' on abortion. Here's why that's ironic http://www.theblaze.com/blog/2015/04/27/hillaryclinton-says-religious-beliefs-have-to-be-changed-on-abortion-heres-why-thats-ironic/Hillary's Campaign Has Already Begun to Derail http://www.nationalreview.com/article/423462/hillarys-campaign-has-already-begun-derail-victor-davis-hanson

FACT RELEASES ITS LIST OF WORST ETHICS VIOLATORS OF 2015 http://www.factdc.org/#!FACT-RELEASES-ITS-LIST-OF-WORST-ETHICS-VIOLATORS-OF-2015/c24/567846da0cf203da56e7450b

FileGate https://fas.org/irp/congress/1996_rpt/fbirep.htm

TravelGate http://www.cnn.com/ALLPOLITICS/1996/news/9605/09/travel.flap/index.shtml

Robert Ray "Final Report of the Independent Counsel of Matters Related to the White House Travel Office http://a255.g.akamaitech.net/7/255/2422/13may20041504/icreport.access.gpo.gov/watkins/86-185.pdf

Woodrow Wilson, Theodore Roosevelt, Franklin Roosevelt, Harry Truman, John F Kennedy, Lyndon B Johnson
www.wikipedia.org

Senate Voting Records and Senate Bill Content:
www.VoteSmart.Org

Jonathan Gruber

https://en.wikipedia.org/wiki/Jonathan_Gruber_(economist)

http://FoxNews.com

www.YouTube.com

About the "basic exploitation" of American voters
https://www.youtube.com/watch?v=t7IlKhqJPH8

GRUBER: "Lack of transparency is a huge political advantage."
https://www.youtube.com/watch?v=G790p0LcgbI

GRUBER: "American voters are too stupid to understand the difference"
https://www.youtube.com/watch?v=iUOyqw5HhRI

House Oversight Committee Grills Jonathan Gruber
https://www.youtube.com/watch?v=6ELvd_bCKb

Civilian Conservation Corp

https://en.wikipedia.org/wiki/Civilian_Conservation_Corps

Other Political News and Commentary

www.foxnews.com

State Department and Libya

Chronology of Libya's Disarmament and Relations with the United States
https://www.armscontrol.org/factsheets/LibyaChronology

The United States and Libya – Foreign Affairs Magazine 1987
https://www.foreignaffairs.com/articles/libya/1986-12-01/unitedstatesandLibya

Muammar Gaddafi
https://en.wikipedia.org/wiki/Muammar_Gaddafi

WikiLeaks
Julian Assange Blasts New York Times And Bill Keller In Rolling Stone Profile
http://www.huffingtonpost.com/2012/01/18/julian-assange-new-york-times-bill-keller-rolling-stone_n_1214361.html

WikiLeaks' War on Secrecy: Truth's Consequences
http://content.time.com/time/magazine/article/0,9171,2034488-1,00.html

Socialism and Obama Care
Blog of Brian Sussman - Conservative Radio Talk show Host. (KSFO)
http://www.briansussman.com/politics/how-obamacare-became-law

Cato Institute: War on Poverty Turns 50: Are We Winning Yet?
http://www.cato.org/publications/policy-analysis/war-poverty turns 50-are-we-winning-yet

http://object.cato.org/sites/cato.org/files/pubs/pdf/pa761_2.pdf

McCarthy, Justin (22 June 2015). "In U.S., Socialist Presidential Candidates Least Appealing".   Gallup.com
http://www.gallup.com/poll/183713/socialist-presidential-candidates-least-appealing.aspx?g_source=In%20US%20Socialist%20Presidential&g_medium=search&g_campaign=tiles

https://en.wikipedia.org/wiki/History_of_the_socialist_movement_in_the_United_States

Theodore Roosevelt

TR, The Story of Theodore Roosevelt, Film Documentary
http://www.pbs.org/wgbh/americanexperience/films/tr/

The Rise of Theodore Roosevelt – Edmund Morris, Modern Library; 3rd Thus edition (2001)

<u>Bill Clinton Impeachment</u>
http://www.washingtonpost.com/wp-srv/politics/special/clinton/stories/impeach122098.htm

The History Channel: This Day in History Dec 19, 1998
http://www.history.com/this-day-in-history/president-clinton-impeached

The History Place : Presidential Impeachment Proceedings
http://www.historyplace.com/unitedstates/impeachments/clinton.htm

The New York Times
http://www.nytimes.com/1998/12/20/us/impeachmentoverview-clinton-impeached-he-faces-senate-trial-2d-history-vows-job.html

Dale Bumpers remembered, his impassioned Senate speech helped save Clinton from conviction
http://www.foxnews.com/politics/2016/01/02/dale-bumpers-remembered-his-impassioned-senate-speech-helped-save-clinton-from-impeachment.html

ABOUT THE AUTHOR

Joseph V McCauley, MBA, has spent his career as a Sr. Supply Chain and IT consultant to high-technology companies such as Cisco Systems, Hewlett Packard, and Apple Computer in California's Silicon Valley. An avid student of history and a life-long Conservative Mr. McCauley is also an ordained minister and the author of two other books: "The Gifts that Reveal God", and "The Any Christian Can Heal Guidebook." Mr. McCauley lives in Virginia Beach, Virginia.

Joseph V. McCauley

www.ingramcontent.com/pod-product-compliance
Lightning Source LLC
Chambersburg PA
CBHW072200280526
45788CB00002B/813